THE
HOMESCHOOL
BOOM

The Homeschool Boom: Pandemic, Policies, and Possibilities—
Why Parents Are Choosing to Homeschool Their Children

Lance Izumi

October 2021

ISBN: 978-1-934276-46-4

Pacific Research Institute
680 E. Colorado Blvd., Suite 180
Pasadena, CA 91101

Tel: 415-989-0833
Fax: 415-989-2411
www.pacificresearch.org

THE HOMESCHOOL BOOM

Pandemic, Policies, and Possibilities—

Why Parents Are Choosing to Homeschool Their Children

LANCE IZUMI

For Rikio, Mikuri, and Rick Izumi

To be raised in a wonderful family is one of the greatest blessings that God can bestow.

CONTENTS

INTRODUCTION

Virtually overnight, the COVID-19 pandemic forced millions of children to receive their education at home as nearly all schools in the United States closed to in-person instruction.

However, the ineffectiveness of the public schools in providing quality distance learning through Zoom and other similar programs not only resulted in significant student learning losses, but also convinced many parents that trying to replicate public school at home, with a one-size-fits-all curriculum and a teacher in charge of a whole classroom, was a failure. For the first time, parents saw with their own eyes why their children were not learning.

In response, many parents started to consider homeschooling, which allowed them to choose the best curriculum, the best learning methods, the best scheduling, the best groupings, and the best services for their children. Rather than having regular public schools dictate what their children had to learn, parents discovered that homeschooling allowed them to have choices about what worked best for their children.

Parents then found that there is a wealth of resources available to homeschoolers, from online curricula to learning videos to various types of neighborhood homeschooling groups to homeschooling arrangements with charter schools.

Parents realized that they did not need a large bureaucratic and often unresponsive system like the regular public schools to educate their children. They found that with the freedom to address the individual needs of their children they were much better able to educate them.

They also found that homeschooling provided their children with a safer environment. They would also be able to promote their family's values and ensure healthier social relationships for their children.

As the COVID-19 pandemic continued, the number of families opting out of the public schools in favor of homeschooling skyrocketed.

This book profiles a diverse group of parents, children, educators, and policy advocates—many who shared their experience with me about homeschooling. Most of the homeschooling students and parents profiled in this book made the shift to homeschooling their kids long before the COVID-19 pandemic. Like new homeschool families during the pandemic, these parents also went through their own trial-and-error process as they searched for what worked best. Eventually, the parents you will meet on these pages figured out a learning model that fulfilled the individual needs of their kids.

Of all the educational choice options available to parents and their children, homeschooling is probably the most misunderstood alternative with the greatest number of myths that have grown up around it.

The myths that swirl around homeschooling are well known. For example, many people think that homeschooling isolates children because they only have contact with their parents, who teach them. As a corollary, it is believed that parents shoulder the entire teaching responsibility with no assistance from any other source.

Also, many believe that homeschooling is practiced by only a narrow demographic of American society.

In terms of curriculum and teaching methods, it is often believed that homeschoolers are taught through rote memorization—the much-disparaged "drill and kill" method—that many claim results in one-dimensional students unable to think critically or deeply.

As to the motivation for homeschooling, the common belief is that families mainly homeschool for religious and moral reasons.

When it comes to children with special needs, it is assumed that parents cannot homeschool such children because they lack the targeted resources that a public school may have available.

Some people, especially influential academics, believe that children are safer if they are taught in schools rather than at home.

As the experiences of millions of parents who became homeschooling parents overnight has shown, these and other widely held views of homeschooling are myths. Not only do recent data debunk these myths, so do the real-life experiences of the people involved in homeschooling.

Throughout the book, the parents, students, and education leaders we interviewed offer advice for parents looking to homeschool their kids full-time. They also share the books, support groups, and other resources they relied upon in becoming homeschoolers, and also give an up-close look at how current public policy affects the homeschooling community.

The reality is that homeschooling is an incredibly diverse movement. The people, the methods, the motives, and the challenges and successes are as varied as the individuals who homeschool.

If there is any common thread that weaves through much of the homeschool movement, it is well captured by Kennesaw State University professor Eric Wearne.

Professor Wearne, who is the author of a well-regarded book on hybrid homeschooling, has pointed out that the growth in homeschooling can be attributed to changes in American life and how people feel about their public schools.

"The growing desire," Wearne has observed, "for smaller and more personalized tastes Americans have developed over the last 20 or so years, enabled (or perhaps driven) in part by improvements in technology, has surely been a major factor."[1]

Thus, "As society is changing—looking for quicker, more bespoke, individualized solutions to everything—technology is changing as well, enabling more creative forms of schooling and making it more accessible."[2] Further:

> American society is more willing to see people working from home making new schooling models logistically plausible. As technology improves and policy evolves to keep up, more individualized models of school choice are be-

coming possible. Schooling models that were somewhat difficult to manage not long ago—homeschooling, online schooling, etc.—have become easier with an increase in the amount of curricular materials available . . . .[3]

In addition, "Families are being 'pushed' out of increasingly large public schools, in a sense, because they feel less welcome there and less able to control or even monitor their children's education."[4]

"To the extent they recognize that students are individually different, with very different needs and interests," says Wearne, the public schools "tend to simply increase in size and complexity to address those differences" and the machinery "only gets bigger."[5]

The result, according to Wearne, is that public schools "in many places have ceased performing their function as mediating institutions, tempered by local preferences and serving as buffers between families and large formal agencies, and simply become larger and larger and more impersonal 'institutions.'"[6]

As a consequence of these two important factors and fueled by the massive educational disruption brought about by the COVID-19 pandemic, homeschooling has transformed from a tiny curious sideshow to an increasingly diverse, innovative, and mainstream part of the education landscape.

Observers across the cultural spectrum have recognized this change.

Wired.com, for instance, has noted, "Technology hasn't just helped a more diverse set of parents start to homeschool—it has given parents a curricular blank canvas, free from the parameters of institutionalized education."[7]

Khadija Ali-Coleman, co-founder of Black Family Homeschool Educators and Scholars, which has grown from a small Facebook group to more than a thousand members, has observed, "what parents are finding is this level of flexibility that doesn't exist within these traditional school settings."[8]

Robin Lake, director of the Center on Reinventing Public Education (CRPE) at the University of Washington, Bothell, and Travis Pillow, a senior fellow at CRPE, have noted:

> A growing infrastructure has made opting out of traditional schooling more feasible. Online resources make it easier for parents to find effective curricula. Parents who don't feel equipped to teach AP Calculus can enroll their students in a part-time online course.
>
> [Homeschool] Co-ops allow parents to curate courses, enrichment opportunities and chances for students to socialize. Microschools and part-time schools offer lower-cost alternatives to private school. Homeschool assistance programs let parents supplement their at-home instruction with courses taught by licensed teachers.[9]

A CRPE analysis of homeschooling found, "The diversity of homeschoolers in the U.S. mirrors the diversity of all students nationally," with the homeschool community including "Muslim and Jewish families, military families, families of gifted students and of those with special needs." In addition, "Homeschoolers run the political spectrum from left to right and the economic spectrum from wealthy to poor." "Regardless of demographics," the analysis observed, "homeschooling families are finding new ways to organize and are blurring the line between traditional school and homeschool."[10]

The parents, children, and educators profiled in this book epitomize this new wave of homeschoolers. They have taken the opportunities offered by technology, varied models of homeschooling, new and abundant curricular resources, and the freedom to personalize learning to meet the needs of those receiving their education outside the traditional classroom.

Their stories will hopefully inspire countless Americans who for whatever reason are dissatisfied with the current direction of their children's education to make a once-unthinkable choice for many, brought about by a global pandemic – the choice to homeschool their kids.

CHAPTER ONE
How Many and Why?

HOW MANY

If the observation is correct that the education environment has ripened so that homeschooling is now much more attractive and much more doable for parents, then one would expect to see a rise in the number of families choosing the homeschool option. In fact, that is exactly what the numbers confirm.

In 1990, there were around 300,000 children being homeschooled in the United States. Thirty years later, the number of homeschoolers had skyrocketed.

In 2021, the United States Census Bureau released a report, the Household Pulse Survey, showing a dramatic increase in the number of homeschoolers across America.[11]

Steven Duvall, research director for the Homeschool Legal Defense Association, analyzed the Census Bureau data and found that by the end of 2020 the number of parents homeschooling their children was 5 million. Given previous federal data showing that 72 percent of families have more than one child at home, Duvall estimated that in excess of 8 million children are being homeschooled.[12]

Not only has the absolute number of homeschoolers grown over the decades, but the rate of growth has also exploded since the advent of the COVID-19 pandemic.

According to Census Bureau researchers, "the global COVID-19 pandemic has sparked new interest in homeschooling and the appeal of alternative school arrangements has suddenly exploded."[13]

At the start of the pandemic, in late April to early May 2020, just over 5 percent of American households reported homeschooling school-aged children. By fall 2020 that percentage had more than doubled to 11 percent reporting homeschooling children. Importantly, the Census Bureau used clarifying information on the Survey to ensure that households were reporting true homeschooling and not distance or remote learning through a public or private school.[14]

At the state level, the jump in homeschooling was eye opening and these increases occurred in both red and blue states.

The percentage of homeschooling households in Florida went from 5 percent to 18 percent, while New York went from 1 percent to 10 percent. Mississippi went from 3 percent to 14 percent, while Massachusetts went from 1.5 percent to 12 percent. Oklahoma went from 8 percent to 20 percent, while Vermont went from 4 percent to 17 percent.[15]

Joy Pulliam, executive editor of *The Federalist*, looked at these increases and commented:

> Once this exodus starts, it will be hard to stop. Parents have for years told pollsters that private education is their top choice, not public education. They haven't left yet because it hasn't gotten bad enough. Long-term coronavirus schooling is easily a tipping point towards 'bad enough to finally leave.' It will likely create a cascade effect of long-term parental divestment from public schooling.[16]

The Census Bureau researchers came to a similar, if more diplomatic, conclusion. "It is clear that in an unprecedented environment," they wrote, "families are seeking solutions that will reliably meet their health and safety needs, their childcare needs and the learning and socio-emotional needs of their children."[17]

Thus, "From the much-discussed 'pandemic pods,' (small groups of students gathering outside a formal school setting for in-person instruction) to a reported influx of parent inquiries about stand-alone virtual schools, private schools and homeschooling organizations, American parents are increasingly open to options beyond the neighborhood school."[18]

Oregon mom Kathleen Bustamante was one of the millions of parents whose experience is captured in the Census Bureau data and who decided to homeschool her children in the wake of the COVID-19 pandemic:

> Our family survived the spring, but as fall 2020 crept closer, I realized Oregon schools would remain virtual for the foreseeable future. So, I decided to invest in a homeschool

curriculum and serve as [my children's] primary educator. The decision was a terrifying one. Although I am a teacher by profession, my only classroom experience has been among adults. I felt ill-equipped to teach my own children: still, I joined the throngs of Americans who pulled their kids from traditional school to give homeschooling a try.[19]

"While COVID-19 disrupted the lives of millions, it also delivered a surprising blessing," said Bustamante. The pandemic has allowed parents to go from being mere observers of their children's education to at-home educators of their children, which "has illuminated the innate ability of parents to effectively teach their children well and produce a new generation of intelligent, capable human beings."[20]

So, if legions of parents are making the decision to homeschool their children, why are they doing so?

THE WHY

Part of the reason surely has to do with the failure of many regular public schools to ensure anything close to adequate learning for students, both during and prior to the COVID-19 pandemic.

A July 2021 study by McKinsey & Company found that by the end of the 2020-21 school year students were "on average five months behind in mathematics and four months behind in reading."[21]

"The pandemic widened preexisting opportunity and achievement gaps, hitting historically disadvantaged students hardest," observed the study's authors. In math, "students in majority Black schools ended the year with six months of unfinished learning, students in low-income schools with seven."[22]

A study by the Center for Research on Education Outcomes at Stanford University looked at regular public school students in 19 states during the COVID-19 pandemic and estimated a loss of 57 to 183 days of learning in reading and 136 to 232 days of learning in math.[23]

In Ohio, a study by researchers at The Ohio State University found that achievement by public school third graders in English language arts had declined by a third of a year's worth of learning from fall 2019 to fall 2020.[24]

In California, one of the first comprehensive studies on the state of student learning in the COVID era was released in January 2021 by the research organization PACE, which is sponsored by the University of California at Los Angeles, the University of Southern California, the University of California at Davis, Stanford University, and the University of California at Berkeley.

The PACE study examined 18 school districts across California and analyzed English and math test scores of students.[25]

The study found that there was significant learning loss in both English and math in the early grades among students.[26]

Further, there was significantly more learning loss from Fall 2019 to Fall 2020 compared to previous years for students from socio-economically disadvantaged backgrounds, particularly in English.[27]

It should be pointed out that even before the pandemic the level of proficiency in the basic subjects among public school students was low.

For example, on the National Assessment for Educational Progress, which is often referred to as the nation's report card, just 34 percent of students taking the 2019 NAEP eighth grade reading exam scored at the proficient level, which is defined as demonstrating competency over the subject matter. The proportion of eighth graders scoring at proficiency in 2019 was a drop of 3 percent compared to results in 2017.[28]

Similarly, only 34 percent of eighth graders taking the 2019 NAEP math exam performed at the proficient level.[29]

Given the overall poor state of learning in regular public schools, which has been exacerbated by the pandemic school closures, many parents have gravitated to homeschooling because it is often believed that homeschoolers achieve at higher levels. Is this view true, however?

The best available research shows this is largely true.

In her 2019 review of the academic research on homeschooling outcomes, Lindsey Burke, director of the Center for Education Policy at the Heritage Foundation, found 26 studies that addressed the academic outcomes of K-12 homeschoolers. Out of these 26 studies, she found, "15 studies reported mainly positive findings, with homeschoolers largely outperforming their non-homeschooled counterparts; nine studies were mixed or neutral in their findings; and two had negative or worse outcomes for homeschooled students relative to their non-homeschooled peers."[30]

Certain states showed particularly strong academic performance by homeschooled students. In Oregon, for instance, "homeschooled students' median percentile range on state standardized tests was between the 71st and 80th percentile." Overall, Burke noted, "Data from state departments of education also show that the median percentile range for homeschooled students on standardized tests of academic achievement is above that of their non-homeschool peers."[31]

"On the whole, the literature suggests students who homeschool have strong academic outcomes," concluded Burke.[32]

It is important to point out, however, that while some parents make the decision to homeschool based on academic performance concerns regarding the regular public schools, many others make this critical decision based on a wide range of factors and considerations. In fact, as Burke acknowledges, "these reasons vary from family to family."[33]

According to federal survey data, the most cited reason given by parents for homeschooling their children is concern about the environment of schools. These concerns include safety, drugs, and negative peer pressure. The second most cited reason is dissatisfaction with the academic instruction at schools. Desire to provide religious instruction trailed those top two reasons.[34]

Lists of reasons why parents decide to homeschool emphasize the diversity of parent motivations. For example, before the pandemic, *Business Insider* listed some top reasons why parents choose homeschooling:

- **Personalized learning is a strong method of instruction.** The core idea of homeschooling is the idea that kids need to learn at the speed, and in the style, most appropriate for them.

- **Students can learn more about what they really care about.** Without formal [school-mandated] curricula to guide their education, homeschoolers get the chance to explore a range of topics that might not be normally offered until high school or college. They can study psychology in the fourth grade, or finance in eighth grade.

- **Students don't deal with cliques or bullying.** Homeschoolers don't deal with all the downsides of being around kids in a toxic school environment. Plenty of critics argue these downsides are actually good for toughening kids up, but kids who are bullied more often face symptoms of depression and anxiety, do worse in class, and show up to school less frequently. Homeschooled kids are able to learn in a more harmonious environment.

- **Schooling isn't set apart from the "real world."** Contrary to the name, homeschooling takes place in an actual home only a fraction of the time. A great deal of instruction happens in community colleges, at libraries, or in the halls of local museums. These experiences have the effect of maturing kids much more quickly and cultivating "a trait of open-mindedness."

- **Students may achieve more in the long run.** Research suggests homeschooled children tend to do better on standardized tests, stick around longer in college, and do better once they're enrolled.[35]

Robin Lake and Travis Pillow of the Center on Reinventing Public Education have noted that parents have unique motivations to homeschool. "They might be desperate to escape bullying, racism or school environments ill-suited to children with special needs," or "they might see value in creating a learning environment where younger children learn from older brothers and sisters." Further, "Perhaps families want to unlock learning experiences, like cross-country road trips, afternoon trips to the museum or immersion in the arts, that don't fit neatly into a traditional school schedule."[36]

Such reasoning has become accentuated in the wake of COVID-19 and its effects on conventional schooling and on students. "COVID-19 was the publicist for homeschooling," notes Khadija Ali-Coleman, co-founder of Black Family Homeschool Educators and Scholars.[37]

As more and more parents started to homeschool their children, they found that homeschooling had immediate impacts on their kids. Steven Duvall, the research director for Homeschool Legal Defense Association, has pointed out:

> It seems reasonable that when the virus led millions of parents across the country to invest in the education of their children to a greater degree than ever before [through homeschooling], many of them likely observed their teens experiencing better mental health . . . making quicker academic gains at home than they experienced in traditional schools . . . feeling safer and more relaxed [and] enjoying tailor-made curricula, learning environments, and flexible time schedules.[38]

The parents, children, and educators profiled in the following chapters epitomize the diversity of individuals involved in homeschooling and the reasons why homeschooling has taken off in popularity.

CHAPTER TWO
How Homeschooling Can Boost Minority Students

One of the biggest stereotypes of homeschooling families is that they are virtually all white. The data, however, shows that this perception is entirely false.

The Census Bureau reports that homeschooling rates "are increasing across race groups and ethnicities." Among African American households in 2020, "the proportion homeschooling increased by five times, from 3.3% (April 23-May 5) to 16.1% in the fall (Sept. 30-Oct. 12)."[39]

Among Hispanic households, the proportion homeschooling their children doubled from more than 6 percent to more than 12 percent. Significant, but somewhat smaller, increases were seen among Asian Americans and whites.[40]

The reasons for this skyrocketing increase in homeschooling among minority groups during the pandemic are many.

For example, the academic inadequacies of the regular public schools during COVID-19 have had a disproportionate impact on minority children. Academic performance indicators have highlighted this disturbing fact.

In Ohio, while third graders overall lost a third of a year's worth of learning in English, African American third graders lost half a year's worth of learning.[41]

Another indicator of students experiencing learning problems is the increase in failing grades. In the Los Angeles Unified School District, data has shown that during the pandemic Latino, African American, English learners, students with disabilities, foster youth, and those experiencing homelessness had double-digit increases in the percentage of Ds and Fs in fall 2020 from the previous year at the same time.[42]

Of course, it is well known that public schools were failing to raise learning rates among African Americans and Latinos prior to the pandemic.

There are other reasons for the rise in homeschooling among minorities besides just poor learning results.

University of Georgia professor of education Cheryl Fields-Smith, perhaps the nation's top expert on homeschooling in the African American community, found a wide array of reasons why African American parents decide to homeschool their children:

> A lot of these families that I interviewed lived in communities where schools had become predominantly black. Their question was, how does my child get a diverse perspective of the world if everything is black? That was some of the rationale, but there were a lot of reasons.

Focus on the test. A certain part of my population tried kindergarten and realized there was too much pencil and paper, not enough learning through play and letting the children be children. About 11 of the 46 [mothers she interviewed in her research] chose to homeschool from birth. They knew the minute they got pregnant that that was what they wanted to do because they felt that they should be their child's first teacher.[43]

Professor Fields-Smith, who is African American, cited safety and labeling as key reasons cited by African American parents for their decision to homeschool. Some of the children of the parents she interviewed for her research "were assigned to a school that had reports of violence, so [they had] safety concerns" and a predominant theme "was a sense of wanting to protect their children from being labeled a troublemaker, or suggestions that they should be in special ed, or even [schools not] acknowledging the intellect of their child because they are so focused on the behavior."[44]

In studying African American homeschoolers, Fields-Smith said, "The diversity within the group surprised me." Indeed, her research exploded the myth of who homeschools their children:

If you look at the broad literature, there is a suggestion that highly religious people homeschool. There is a suggestion that people who are anti-government homeschool. There is a suggestion that affluent people homeschool. In my study, it completely shows the opposite. Out of 46 families, only four of them had advanced degrees. I had families who had no postsecondary education. I had some that had some college. A lot of them had bachelor's degrees. For some of them, I got the sense that they were really sacrificing that second income. That meant [they had] to hang on to a car a lot longer than they normally would, or furniture a lot longer . . . . Instead of being a solid middle-class family with two incomes . . . they were more working class or working middle class.[45]

The same diversity characterizes the rise in homeschooling among Hispanics. According to the publication *redefineED*:

Hispanic home school parents interviewed by *redefineED* cited many of the same factors as other homeschool parents. Safety. Negative influences. Too much testing. They said Hispanic families want more flexibility to balance school and family. They want more emphasis on character and faith.[46]

The publication found that the burgeoning number of resources available to homeschooling families, including Hispanic homeschoolers, means "they don't have to go it alone." The Hispanic parents interviewed "noted the growth of co-ops and other resources that can orient newcomers and supplement their educational programs."[47]

One Hispanic parent interviewed by the publication described the influence of Hispanic culture on the rise of homeschooling's popularity: "We are such family-oriented people. We are all about being together." After describing how multi-generations of adults can assist in homeschooling her children, she said, "If there's a rise [in Hispanic homeschoolers], I think that's part of it."[48]

As homeschooling becomes a significant part of the education landscape in the Hispanic community, Hispanic homeschoolers have started new groups to help families start and continue their homeschooling journeys.

For example, Monica Olivera, a homeschooling mother of three, started a blog called Mommy Maestra, where she provides "resources for Latino homeschoolers that I was slowly discovering through my own journey as a Latina homeschooling mom."[49]

In 2020, in the midst of the COVID pandemic, Olivera launched a Facebook group called Hispanic & Bilingual Homeschoolers, which she said was a way to fill the gap in the Hispanic community for "one national group where we can ask questions and get support from each other," such as "where to find bilingual materials, how to incorporate culture into our lessons, where to find co-ops with other Hispanic or Latino families, and how to find basic homeschool information."[50]

In less than a year, Olivera's Facebook group had 2500 members.

As one Hispanic mom summed up, "More Hispanic families are thinking, 'I can do this.'"[51]

So who are some of these minority homeschoolers that the data and the experts indicate are a significant part of the homeschool movement? In this chapter, we meet two amazing minority homeschool parents.

MAGDA GOMEZ

"I was born in Tijuana, Mexico," says Magda Gomez. As a teenager, "One of my first challenges was to migrate to [the United States] with no English."

People who think that only wealthy whites homeschool their children should meet Magda. Like many immigrants to America, she learned English as an English-as-a-second-language student in high school in California. She had to work almost full-time—30 to 35 hours a week—as a cashier at a 24-hour restaurant at the age of 16.

"I knew my parents were not going to be able to pay for my college tuition," she recalled, "and I was determined to attend college."

Her passion was for acting, which she pursued as a student at Santa Ana College, a community college in Southern California, and later through a drama group in Spanish at the Crystal Cathedral in Garden Grove and various theater groups in the Los Angeles area.

Gomez graduated from Santa Ana College with an associate of arts degree and then enrolled at California State University Long Beach. However, due to a variety of personal setbacks, including a divorce and the loss of her house, she had to drop out.

Despite these challenges, she has been able to raise two wonderful daughters, Lilian, who is now 18, and Vanessa, who is 13. And, she says, "One of the things I feel most proud about is having taken the decision to homeschool my two daughters."

She did not start homeschooling her girls at the beginning, however. Lilian went to a regular public school from kindergarten through the sixth grade, while Vanessa went to a traditional public school from kindergarten to the first grade and to a charter school in the second grade.

Lilian is an accomplished student. When she was in the third grade, Gomez remembered, Lilian took a school placement test. A school official told Gomez that her daughter was the only student in his ten years of experience who had ever finished the entire exam. In addition, Lilian got every answer correct.

In the fifth grade, Lilian ran for class president. "Even though she didn't win," Gomez observed, "I can tell you I truly see her as president of the United States." Watching her daughter be recognized at a school assembly for her run for class president, Gomez noted, "Sadly, at that school, most Hispanic students were not the ones succeeding at their classes."

Her youngest daughter Vanessa is equally accomplished. In public school, she received awards, won spelling bee competitions, scored well on tests, and moved into first grade when she was only five years old.

Despite her children's accomplishments, Gomez was not satisfied with their public schools.

"I thought about homeschooling five years before I started doing it," she said. "I never liked the school system we have here" because "when I came from Tijuana, I could compare the two education systems."

In Mexico, "teachers expected students to be mature and responsible, and we were." "Here," however, "they expect the students to be immature and irresponsible, and they are, or at least most of them."

She related how her children, despite their academic accomplishments, "were always the ones who other girls or boys would pick on." She gave a number of examples.

When Lilian was in the third grade a boy tried pulling down her pants twice during recess. When Vanessa was in the first grade, another girl was hitting her virtually every day and "One day, she was about to poke her eye with a pencil."

Her daughters never fought back since Gomez had always told them, "the right way to deal with this kind of situation in school was always to go to their teacher for help." But "it was hard to keep up with all of these children's bad behavior."

> I guess all what I'm trying to say with all these stories is I decided to homeschool because my daughters were already doing great even before starting kindergarten. They were well-behaved girls inside and outside of school. I never depended on the school system to educate my daughters. And to keep on sending my daughters to school just to receive the academic portion was not worth it when at the same time they were being hurt by other students.

Gomez knew she could homeschool her daughters. "I was always one of the top students in school," she said. She also thought that homeschooling would offer more flexibility with the family's acting interests:

> Another reason for us to homeschool is that we are very involved in theatre. [Lilian and Vanessa] both have been on stage since they were one year old. Before 2020, we were presenting at least two musicals a year, one in

English and one in Spanish. Plus, I was being hired as a stage manager for at least three different events throughout the year where my daughters were also on stage, too. Learning a script and rehearsals are time consuming. Sometimes they go to bed late during a school day. But doing homeschool means we chose our own time. We use the flexibility of homeschooling to create a schedule that works best for our family.

There are a number of different options when it comes to homeschooling, but she used a private school affidavit (PSA) to homeschool her children. According to the California Department of Education, homeschool parents file a PSA if their children are not enrolled in a public or private elementary or secondary school and if they are providing instruction to their children who are not enrolled in such schools.[52] In other words, she independently homeschooled her children acting as her own private school.

Gomez felt capable of teaching her own children since she had graduated from community college. Teachers, she said, "go to a one-year program that teaches them to teach a group of children." "Parents don't need that" since "we know our own children" and "once we become parents, we become teachers." Further, she had gained experience working for a family support program and receiving training in child development and working in various roles at regular public and charter schools.

Besides the schedule flexibility offered by homeschooling, she said that educating her daughters at home allowed her to control their nutrition by giving them healthy meals; customize their curriculum by allowing extra time for subjects that really interest her children; give them the opportunity to socialize in a variety of settings with people of different ages, not just their age-level peers; and ensure one-on-one instruction and assistance from her.

Of course, homeschooling is not always a smooth ride. There are bumps along the way. While her daughters usually do not complain about things, occasionally they will voice objections to why they have to do this or that.

"Of course, I try to keep them motivated," she says, "I go back and explain why we are doing this—family values, faith, family goals, and personal talents like theater."

"At the end of the day, I love my children and treat them with respect," she says, but "I am the adult. I want to raise happy successful citizens."

Schools, she observes, do not teach these things in the classroom. Through homeschooling, she can see the progress being made by her youngest daughter reading on her own every night "just because a book is very interesting and now is a habit for her" or "deciding to switch their whole conversation to Spanish when her grandma arrives to show respect to her."

Yes, her children will make mistakes, but she says, "It is my job to continue observing every day all their little actions and intervene if they are wrong."

She has definite ideas about homeschooling and its role and potential in the Hispanic community. And she is active in guiding Hispanic parents in making and evaluating education options.

"Most [immigrant parents]," she says, "feel nervous and are afraid they will get in trouble."

"At the beginning," given the lack of information and the experiences they have had in their native countries, "they think it is illegal or they feel they might need their child's school's permission."

She runs Broadway Productions, which promotes theater in Spanish. She created a program called "Se Abre El Telon Con Magda," which produces videos and parenting classes where "we educate Hispanic parents about our right to choose public quality education for our children."

She talks to parents whose children are in regular public schools and "If their children are not being successful in their current school, that's when I guide them more about all these other options."

Due to school closures resulting from COVID-19, many Hispanic parents were exposed to online education. According to Gomez, for the first time many Hispanic parents have seen that their children can handle online learning and she hopes to see more Hispanic families opt for homeschooling.

She realizes that not all Hispanic parents can homeschool. For example, if a parent has a child with behavior issues such as drug use, she "will refer this family to local charters where they have more one-to-one or small group classes, counselors, and experienced teachers."

Referring to one of her videos, which she narrates in Spanish and which she directs at Hispanic homeschooling parents, she says: "We Hispanics as a culture are usually very protective and loving towards our children. However, I explain that love is not enough to raise our children. We have to educate ourselves in different areas [of education], especially since we are not in our [native] country but are immigrants."

In addition to her videos, she plans to reach Hispanic parents through a musical event, planned for 2022, entitled "Mi Educacion Mi Opcion el Musical//School Choice the Musical," which will be done in Spanish. The musical "will be about the urgency for the Hispanic parents living in the U.S. to learn more about school choice if their children are not being successful in their traditional public school."

Gomez's life story is the quintessentially American story of an immigrant who came to this country seeking a better life and not only finding it, but also working hard to make life better for others, especially in her own community.

"I continue giving back to the community by helping kids, teenagers, and adults," she says. "It is my dream to see more Hispanic families doing homeschool."

DEMETRIA ZINGA

In an article entitled "10 Black Homeschool Moms You Should Follow," Mater Mea, a website that "celebrates, supports, and empowers Black Moms," recommended: "Whether you're considering homeschooling, just starting out, or are a veteran homeschooler, here are some of the best Black homeschoolers to follow online."[53] One of those top 10 homeschoolers is Demetria Zinga.

In its profile of her, the website article said, "Demetria of the blog and Youtube channel Mom Zest (https://momzest.com) is a down-to-earth, homeschooling mama, raising two daughters with her husband in Silicon Valley."[54]

She describes her blog as "a chronicle of my homeschooling journey the past 14 years, choices I've made in my work at raising strong, young black women, and my work at developing my own interests and career choices."[55]

She believes that African American families "choose homeschooling for different reasons" and that "each family is unique." Some choose to homeschool because of the time and schedule flexibility it offers, while others choose it because they want to take their children out of the public schools because their kids "are being dishonored or devalued."

She also emphasizes that some African American parents have made the deliberate decision to homeschool their children from the outset, rather than deciding as a reflex to bad experiences in the public schools.

Demetria is a Christian and says that faith is an integral part of who she is. Further, "faith is important to our whole home life in general." For many years she had a podcast aimed at Christian homeschool moms.

In addition, she says that many African American families want to "share our values and we want to pass on our heritage, which cannot be done holistically if we're sending off our children for eight hours a day to be under the care of a system that doesn't support that."

Part of Zinga's grounded nature probably comes from her family's military ties. She grew up in an Air Force family and was born on an Air Force base in Georgia.

Like most children in military families, she attended school in a wide variety of locales, from England to Montana to Korea to California.

"I actually loved school," she recalled. "I loved everything that came along with school when I was younger." In fact, "I was the one that was always pushing my parents for more because I was kind of an overachiever."

Small children, Demetria observes, "are like sponges and they really have a passion to learn." "It's just that they are free and they want to learn."

She went to the University of Alabama and majored in child development. "I had a passion for teaching kids," she said. "Oh, I loved it," she described, especially "the hands-on lab because we actually got to work with the students."

She contrasts the child development major, where "we were really focused on the developmentally appropriate activities for kids," versus the education major, where the focus was on "how you teach science, how you teach social studies, whatever the subject is," so "it was about uniformity, about the control of subject matter, and also the control of the classroom, and how to deliver content."

After graduating, she worked in the university's engineering library where she met her husband Bob, an immigrant from the Republic of the Congo who worked in the same library system. After getting married, having their first child, getting a master's degree, and starting her own digital business, she gravitated to homeschooling.

Initially, homeschooling was a foreign concept, especially for her husband. They were both geared to more conventional schools, "So we had to really think about what that would mean." Therefore, they weighed all the costs and benefits.

"I actually never heard of homeschooling," recalls Demetria. Once hearing about the concept, she checked out all the books in the library about it.

Because her husband is an officer in the United States Naval Reserve, he traveled a great deal. She thought that homeschooling would allow the family the flexibility to travel together when her husband was on duty. "I love the freedom to just say, 'Okay, I'll go with you,'" she said.

A key benefit had to do with her oldest daughter's personality. Zinga says, "she was a very, very focused and determined young lady from the beginning, so she was determined that she wanted to learn a lot."

For her part, Zinga wanted to teach and just "hang out with her." She taught her daughter reading using phonics videos and other resources. Her daughter learned reading so well that Zinga felt that if she sent her to a regular public school that her daughter would be so advanced "she might be bored and not fit in."

Once the decision to homeschool was made in 2007, "it was important to find a group of people who were similar, so we needed to find a homeschool group." "I didn't want to be out there floating around on my own," she said, so the family joined a local homeschool co-op.

The co-op consisted of a group of homeschool parents who brought their children together once a week and parents would participate and share teaching duties. "So," she says, "you just choose what you're going to offer once a week to your classes."

"All the subjects were available to teach; it was a very organized cooperative, so that was brilliant."

Initially, her homeschooling style of instruction was very structured. But "then I realized after about seven or eight months in homeschool that [structured instruction] really just didn't work for us." Instead, she adopted what she called "relaxed homeschooling," which is between structured instruction and a totally unstructured technique called unschooling (which will be discussed in a later chapter).

Under her relaxed homeschooling method, she was able to mix a curriculum with the interests of her children, allowing them to "explore and take an adventure, but come back to our map." The family eventually moved to California in 2011. She continued to homeschool in the family's new state. She also engaged in various types of homeschooling, including independent homeschooling using a private school affidavit and homeschooling through a charter school.

One of the things that she noted is that homeschooling allows one to choose and discard curriculum choices depending on whether it works for the child. "So," she says, "we might try something for a season and then realize that's not necessarily our style and then try something different."

For quite some time, she used the Charlotte Mason method to instruct her children. Mason was a British education reformer at the turn of the twentieth century who opposed dry textbooks, worksheets, and overly long lessons and homework. Instead, she believed that children should read intellectually nourishing "living books" by the best authors, receive shorter lessons, and narrate their own written or oral works.[56]

"I loved her philosophy," she says, "so I embraced it."

However, the needs of her oldest daughter changed after the family moved to California. So, eventually, she shifted to the Classical Conversations program for homeschoolers.

Classical Conversations provides "weekly classical, Christian communities that hone students' academic and classical skills of recitation, logical thinking, and persuasive rhetoric." In addition, it provides parent practicums "that empower parents to teach any academic subject classically." Also, it provides "a curriculum framework with a Christ-centered worldview while engaging the current culture in which we live."[57]

Demetria says that her oldest daughter Nyomi needed the structure that came with Classical Conversations. Nyomi participated in Classical Conversations during her junior and senior high school years of homeschool.

In one of her YouTube videos, Zinga interviewed her daughter when she graduated from Classical Conversations.

"I like Classical Conversations," said Nyomi, "because you have a lot of discussions and I get to give my opinions." She noted that the program required a lot of books, writing, and reading, "So it can be a pretty hard challenge, really hard." But "it was helpful to make me a better writer."[58] Nyomi graduated from Classical Conversations with honors.

While Nyomi was completing her junior and senior years in Classical Conversations, her sister Zoe completed fifth and sixth grade through the program. Zinga also tutored a Classical Conversations class for a year. She said it "was an absolutely amazing experience—mainly because I enjoy teaching—and I enjoyed my class very much."

However, what is good for one person may not be good for another. So, while Classical Conversations was the right fit for Nyomi, Zoe was a different story.

Zinga found that under the program, subjects such as math, history, and science were not covered enough for middle-school-aged Zoe. Also, Zoe was not interested in debate, which is a big part of Classical Conversations. As an artsy, theatrical, and entrepreneurial person, Zoe did not seem to fit the program well. Finally, Zinga had concerns about various book selections that did not gel with her family's views. So, she took Zoe out of Classical Conversations.

Zinga enrolled her in another classical-education program that used a university model where students met a few times per week and took classes conducted by teachers. The rest of the days of the week were spent in homeschooling.

Zinga herself applied for and was accepted to become an actual teacher at the school. She taught English language arts and history to third graders. She had such a great experience and found that she loved teaching so much that she put on hold all her other activities, from blogging to producing videos to designing websites, in order to follow her teaching passion. After teaching the third graders at the school, she is now teaching preschoolers through Outschool, which offers more than 100,000 interactive online classes.

Looking to the future, Zinga says, "I believe homeschooling is growing and exploding amongst African Americans and there will be more and more homeschoolers." She believes that this homeschooling growth will be "more community centric."

This growth and focus, she believes, will be facilitated by "more resources available, in general, but also with regard to the African-American community, in particular, especially online that would make it easier for people to homeschool."

Despite twists and turns, Zinga says that homeschooling has "been a tremendous journey and a journey well worth it because I experienced that with my family, my kids." "And," she observes, "I really got to be there for them in a way that I wouldn't have been any way else."

CHAPTER THREE
Homeschooling Children with Special Needs

Another big myth about homeschooling is that parents cannot successfully homeschool their children with special needs. Many believe that only credentialed professionals can provide special-needs students the instruction and learning services they need to succeed. In reality, for many parents, it is the deficiency of the public schools in providing effective special-needs education that pushed them to homeschool their special-needs children.

In 2021, the school-choice organization EdChoice commissioned focus groups of homeschoolers: "Many parents of children with autism, ADHD, and other neuro-developmental disorders report that public schools cannot effectively address their child's specialized learning needs and lack sufficient behavioral support services."[59]

Further, "These parents emphasize the need for their children to receive more individualized attention and comprehensive support in order to succeed academically."

One parent of a fifth-grade child with special needs said:

> My 11-year-old has some special needs. He's got autism on the mild end of the spectrum, but still definitely challenging, and some attention deficit issues. He really does need a lot of one-on-one attention. We just weren't seeing that in the school. We decided to pull him out and homeschool him. We didn't feel like we're getting an honest assessment of our son's abilities. We wanted to see with our own eyes, what was he doing, how is he doing.

As opposed to the rigid one-size-fits-all structure that schools often impose on special-needs children, homeschooling allows parents to address the particular individual needs of their child. According to the EdChoice report, "Children with special needs require more parent engagement and flexibility to adapt to homeschool and find a customized system that works."[60]

The report quotes the parent of a kindergartener who says:

> My five-year-old has ADHD, so the schedule is unpredictable. One day, everything would be good. I don't know what I'm going to get with her. She likes to participate, but she's just distracted a lot, so she's got to run outside, do some laps.[61]

In a structured setting like a public school classroom, the ability for this parent's child to just run outside and "do some laps" would be highly unlikely.

Jackie Nunes, a former pediatric nurse, decided to pull her daughter, who had suffered a traumatic brain injury and is developmentally delayed with sensory processing issues, out of her public school and homeschool her instead.[62]

"I grew up in public schools," says Nunes, but "two years ago, I disenrolled my daughter, who has special needs." Although she acknowledged that many teachers are "amazing people," she observed:

> But when there are too many students and not enough staff, too many needs and not enough resources, it's easy to forget that. Sitting around a conference table at an IEP (individualized education plan) meeting can feel like going into battle. In our case, there wasn't any gross negligence, bullying or neglect. There just wasn't enough of the things that matter— time, attention, patience, persistence, passion, support.[63]

"Homeschooling comes with many benefits," Nunes points out, "particularly for children with special needs." She listed four important advantages:

> **One-on-One Focus:** In a traditional classroom setting, teachers often do not have the time or resources to give every child individual attention. In a homeschool situation, however, parents have the ability to teach in a personalized manner all day, every day. Any aspect of education that requires specialized instruction, like reading and writing, math basics or handwriting, can be emphasized for as much time and in as many ways as necessary.

Flexible Scheduling: While it's commonly encouraged for homeschooling parents to stick to a normal school schedule while teaching at home, a home environment offers flexibility that a classroom never can. If your child struggles with focusing, has meltdowns, or has sensory processing issues, you can take breaks as needed to reschedule lessons for a better time. If you have a doctor or therapy appointment, you can work around it.

Creative Curricula: Do you prefer to start the day with math while your child is still fresh and end the day with reading or art when he's running out of steam? When you homeschool, anything is possible. There are no limitations on what you teach, when you teach it or how you choose to teach it, giving you the freedom to explore a curriculum that works for you.

Custom Environment: For children with special needs, a traditional classroom with desks in straight lines and a lot of time spent sitting still and being quiet isn't necessarily a good fit. Not all children can stay still for hours on end, and some are easily overwhelmed by the presence of other children, posters on the walls or blocks and toys. In a homeschool situation, it's up to you to create an atmosphere that works, whether that means a space with plenty of room to run around, a quiet and calm environment free of distractions, or seating options that include beanbags, swings and yoga balls.[64]

Homeschooling a child with special needs does have downsides, such as parental exhaustion, but Nunes says, "For my family, the good has far outweighed the bad."[65] The following are stories of parents who have homeschooled their special-needs children successfully.

CARRIE CARLSON AND GARRETT

In retrospect, it was a harbinger of things to come. Carrie Carlson hated her experience in a public high school in Northern California, especially the social aspect of it. "I remember asking my mom if I could be homeschooled," recalled Carrie. Her mom said no, but years later she was homeschooling her own children, including her son who has special needs.

Despite her dislike of high school, she went on to college, eventually receiving her teaching credential from California State University, Sacramento. She had always wanted to be a teacher, even from a young age.

"I was always teaching," she recalled, and when other kids visited her house for play dates, "I would set up a little school." "When they wouldn't listen to me anymore," she laughed, "I would set up my animals and my dogs and I would teach them."

When she was in her teacher-training program, she does not remember homeschooling being discussed. Regardless, "I definitely was not in favor of it."

She taught in a number of Northern California regular public schools. She found teaching "very rewarding, I really, really loved it."

"I related very well to the kids that were struggling or maybe didn't have a ton of parent support," she said.

In her personal life, she married and had two children, a son and a daughter.

Despite her college-era misgivings about homeschooling and her initial career teaching in public schools, she opened an in-home preschool when her children were preschool age. She ran the preschool for three years and then shut it down when her daughter was no longer preschool age.

She says that her daughter Greta is very self-motivated, driven, and a goal-setter. "She knows exactly what she wants and is a hard worker," she says.

Also, "she's an artist and really passionate about her art and animation."

She describes her son Garrett as a "very kind individual and I think he's probably got one of the warmest hearts." She uses words like "compassionate," "helpful," "unselfish," "empathetic," and "thoughtful" to describe him. "He's a very deep thinker," she observes, "and he's like an old soul."

Garrett is also on the autism spectrum.

It was Garrett who alerted them. One day, she says, he came home from Boy Scouts and said, "I don't think I'm like the other kids." "I always say Garrett led us to his autism diagnosis," she said. It was not until the age of 12 that Garrett was diagnosed as being autistic.

"So, he struggles in social environments," notes Carrie, and "he struggles a bit to understand other people's emotions." Aware of his own autism, Garrett, according to Carrie, will ask people, "'Are you upset right now?' or 'Are you angry?' or 'How can I help?' because he knows that he doesn't read people's emotions very well."

Garrett also has severe dyslexia, "so decoding and reading is still very, very much of a challenge for him." Interestingly, though, content and comprehension are not hard for him.

"So, one of the things that's kind of fascinating about Garrett is that we didn't realize that he had these disabilities until he was eight or nine," she says. In kindergarten, Garrett "couldn't really do even letters or sounds, but he was comprehending . . . at like a 12th-grade level."

Prior to knowing that Garrett was autistic, she and her husband had initially enrolled him in public school kindergarten. While in kindergarten, Garrett developed a stutter and became very anxious. Garrett acknowledges, "I am a little more nervous in classrooms."

Also in kindergarten, his dyslexia became apparent. "It was harder for me to read," says Garrett, although "it wasn't impossible."

She said that he would wake up happy, but then as it got to be closer to the time to get on the bus "he started coming up with ailments as to why he couldn't go to school, like my stomach hurts." One time, "he told us he had prostate cancer, which we thought was hilarious."

Also, in his class, Garrett was always put in the lowest performance group. Further, "the lowest group in his class was Spanish speaking, so he's just sitting in a group where the kids are all speaking Spanish." She asked, "How is this even helping him? Like it doesn't make sense."

The final straw came when Garrett's teacher told her in a parent conference that Garrett was meeting the grade-level standards, but was behind his fellow students. As a teacher, this assessment incensed her.

She told the teacher, "I'm sorry, I don't mean to be disrespectful, but we don't compare students to students, we compare students to standards."

She marched to the principal's office to voice her displeasure. She said that the principal looked at her and said: "I don't ever tell a person to do this, but I can't promise you that I have teachers that are going to cater to your child. I would tell you to homeschool your kids."

"I don't have a teacher that will meet [Garrett's] needs," she recalled the principal admitting.

The next day, Carlson pulled Garrett out of the public school to homeschool him.

The following week, she had set up a little classroom in her house, "and I was like, okay, Garrett, let's get started and let's get taught, and that lasted about three days." "The first day," she said, "it lasted for about 20 minutes," the second day lasted less, "and the third day even less."

While she was trying to teach Garrett, "he literally would roll around on the floor and didn't want to do anything and didn't want to pay attention." It was not that Garrett did not want to do anything, "He just didn't want to do that and he didn't want to do it that way."

"Well, clearly, this isn't going to work," she said.

So, that was when she "started researching anything and everything I could about homeschooling."

At the same time, she took Garrett to see a neurologist who said that her son had "typical development" and "they didn't diagnose him with autism or anything." She was told, however, "he will not learn the same way that other people learn so keep him as far away from schools, teachers, and classrooms as possible."

The neurologist recommended that she take Garrett to museums, take him on field trips, and let him explore the world because that is how he was going to learn.

Since kindergarten is not mandated in California, and after those three days of unsuccessfully trying to teach Garrett on her own, Carrie decided not to start schooling Garrett until he was six and ready for the first grade.

She decided to homeschool Garrett by enrolling him in a non-classroom-based charter school as an independent study student. Non-classroom-based homeschool charter schools will be discussed more thoroughly in Chapter Six.

During the first years of homeschooling, she was a full-time stay-at-home mom.

When Garrett was ready to enter the third grade, she pulled him out of the homeschool charter and decided to homeschool him independently using her own teaching credential.

She explains, "in the state of California, as long as you are credentialed in the subjects and grades of your kids, you can homeschool without filing anywhere and you just have to keep records." "If anyone comes knocking on your door," she says, "you just have to show your credentials."

Carlson might have had a credential, but homeschooling Garrett was not easy. It was especially a struggle to teach him how to read. "So we tried so many different programs," she said, "and we tried so many different platforms to teach him how to read."

However, because homeschooling allows parents to change approaches when they do not succeed, she switched course with reading instruction:

> So we just did what he was interested in. We just explored everything that he was interested in. We went on trips. We did exactly what the neurologist told us to do. So we read together and then because he struggled with decoding, we just quickly transitioned him to audio. He devoured books on audio. I mean, he's actually probably one of the most well read dyslexic kids I've ever met in my life.

When he was eight, Garrett went through the entire mammoth J.R.R. Tolkien trilogy *The Lord of the Rings* on audio books. The trilogy is complicated, but Garrett absorbed it because he had come to love fantasy literature.

Also, "I think that one of the things that has been great about being able to homeschool him is being able to adjust his learning of content to fit his pace." Carlson says, "what has worked for him is going slower, taking things in smaller chunks, and taking a lot of breaks." Garrett can work intensively for 10 to 15 minutes but would then need to take a break. This pattern of short spurts of intense activity followed by breaks works for Garrett, "so having the freedom to be able to do that and not be on a school-bell schedule is important."

If Garrett had been in a regular public school, "I think he would have suffered from a lot more depression and anxiety." In kindergarten Garrett had a stutter and could not sleep, which are signs of anxiety. If he was forced to go through regular public school culminating in a regular public high school, "I think he would have just continued to spiral down, so keeping him out of that environment allowed him to grow on his own and allowed him to find the things that he loves or that he's passionate about." As a result, "he's willing to work hard and advocate for himself and I think that's hugely positive and I don't think he would have done that in a high school environment."

Further, homeschooling works with Garrett's body clock and bodily needs. "He's a sleeper and he sleeps hard and heavy," she says, "and he needs eight to 10 hours of sleep." So, "knowing that he doesn't have to get up at a certain time to be at a certain school on somebody else's schedule has been awesome."

Eventually, for his high school years, Carlson enrolled Garrett in Clarksville Charter School, which is a non-classroom-based homeschool charter school.

So what does Garrett's regular day look like now? According to Carlson, he gets up between eight and nine in the morning, showers, makes breakfast for himself, does morning chores, and takes the family dog on a walk. At 10 AM, "he will start his school work, whatever that might be."

When Garrett takes a course, he will do so much work, then "take a break, go outside, walk around, play with our dog." This pattern of work-then-break is self-directed by Garrett, and she says, "I don't remind him to do anything because he just kind of plans out his own days."

Garrett still has reading issues, so she has to determine how to handle any reading materials associated with a course Garrett may be taking. If the course has audio books, then Garrett will use them. "If not," she says, "I will actually still sit and read to him if it's not an audio book." Garrett can read, "but it's very slow and very labored."

Despite his personal challenges, Garrett is very motivated. "Yeah, it's actually pretty amazing," she says, "I never have to remind him to do anything and every time I see him, he says, 'Oh, I'm working on this right now,' or 'I'm working on that right now.'"

Many people might assume that the success that Garrett has had in his learning is only due to the fact that his mother is a credentialed teacher. Carlson, however, explodes this assumption.

"If anything," she says, "my credential and going through [credentialing] school was more of a hindrance to my being open to the style which we adopted as far as schooling the kids." "I had to do a lot of unlearning," she admitted.

"I had to have a huge paradigm shift on what is education and what does it mean to be educated," she explained. "So, in many ways, all my schooling was actually leading me away from ever thinking that homeschooling was a possibility."

In fact, she believes that if she had not gone through a teacher-training program and did not have a teaching credential she would have been a better homeschooling parent. "I think I would have done a better job because I would have adopted the idea of natural learning much sooner and I wouldn't have had as many internal conflicts," she says.

These internal conflicts were caused by conflicting information. "I've been told all my life that [conventional education] is the only way to learn," she explained, "but I'm seeing just the opposite." She believes that the effort to teach Garrett to read "would have been easier."

When asked about how she would advise parents trying to decide whether to homeschool their special-needs children,

Carrie first says, "if there is any sort of social-emotional reason, pull them out." She warns that the pressures of school and learning at school "are so intense that they're causing huge amounts of depression and anxiety."

"Don't even hesitate," she says, "because I just think there's nothing worth sacrificing that kind of mental health for."

"And don't do anything until it feels right," she says, "because it's not for the faint of heart."

Although he might not score high on some standardized test, Carrie says that she feels more confident in Garrett "walking into the future, and I actually feel better about him going out into the public, than I feel about a lot of kids that have gone through a brick-and-mortar school."

Because of homeschooling, says Garrett, "I'm able to do so much better." "I'm able to take my time, I'm not forced to do everything on a table," he says. He can also make his own schedule. If he was stuck in a traditional public school, Garrett says, "I think I'd be really depressed and would probably have very low self-esteem."

"At the end of the day," Carrie says, "what we really want are kind, well-functioning, and happy people." And Garrett is all of those things.

LOUISA, JAMES, AND THEODORE

"One-size-fits-all doesn't work," says Louisa (her real name and the names of the members of her family have been changed upon her request). Her husband James agreed and pointed to being placed in a new math program back when he was in high school. "My parents didn't have a choice and I didn't have a choice," he says.

Louisa and James have two children. Theodore, their oldest, has special needs.

"He is hearing impaired," says Louisa, "wears hearing aids and he struggles with sensory integration issues and has sensory processing disorders." Specifically, Theodore has hyposensitivity.

A common definition of hyposensitivity is that it "refers to low or abnormally decreased sensitivity to motion and sense of touch." People with hyposensitivity "need a lot more sensation than a normal person does," so whereas a person without hyposensitivity "would spin in circles for a short time, a hyposensitive person would spin for longer periods of time."[66]

Louisa says that Theodore can be twirled like the Tasmanian Devil, the old Warner Brothers cartoon character, "and he actually craves it." "We didn't know it at the time," she says, "but looking back, he craved a lot of physical, huge motion."

As a baby, when Theodore would be thrown in the air by his father, Louisa says, "he wanted more and more and more all the time, so he needed to feel the physical motion."

Part of Theodore's hyposensitivity included not being able to feel his legs and arms in space. Thus, says Louisa, "he would have to have somebody holding on to his arm, squeezing his arms and legs, so he could feel stable in space."

"It's like if you put your arm underneath a table," Louisa explains, "you can't see it, but you know it's there." Theodore, however, "didn't develop that awareness, even though he could see his body, his feet, his hand, he still had no sense of where he was in space."

Further, "he wasn't cognizant of where his body was in relation to other inanimate objects or people."

"My muscles feel tense, and I just want to shout at the top of my lungs and command what I want to happen and what I want to happen will just happen," says Theodore.

Because of his hyposensitivity, Theodore developed behavioral frustrations. Louisa says that he would get worked up and he would feel that things were out of control "in terms of people being scattered, or a lot of energy in a place with a lot of people."

Theodore himself says, "One of my main challenges is when there's a lot of noise, a lot of talking, or a lot of commotion at a big gathering I just get out of whack." He does say, "I feel like I've been able to conquer that challenge a little bit as I've gotten older."

He would talk a great deal and would get very stressed. Theodore would "feel the stress in his body" and, according to Louisa, "he wouldn't know how to process that" and "he was just so incredibly stressed by all this kind of mismatched energy in his body that he would just kind of freak out."

"Sometimes I get frustrated easily," says Theodore, "and sometimes I'll go to my bed and just punch the mattress or the pillow because I feel angry, and I feel like I want to do something to get it out and that calms me down."

Louisa and James started to notice Theodore's challenges when he was a toddler. At first, they chalked up these problems to his young age. However, Theodore's issues became more pronounced as he grew older.

In response, they consulted a number of different professionals, from doctors to occupational therapists. These professionals have focused on giving Theodore the "tools and the therapies needed to make him successful."

Louisa says that today "there's still times, not often, where there are situations where he feels overwhelmed, but we've been working so many years on tools for him to manage it and then he also knows himself." Theodore knows "when he just needs to take a break from the situation so he can manage himself."

Before they realized the extent of Theodore's issues, Louisa and James initially thought that they would send him to school. However, as his issues became more apparent and they received diagnoses from doctors, James says, "we realized he's going to need something different" and that "he's going to need his own specialized focused education."

They talked to one of their neighbors who had a young daughter with autism. This neighbor was homeschooling her daughter because, according to James, "they tried regular school and the school didn't give them anything that they needed for their daughter and her daughter basically sat in the corner all day and did nothing and learned nothing." "She didn't learn anything," he emphasized, "and was very unproductive and did not improve at all."

After hearing about the experience of their neighbor's child, Louisa and James realized that they could not put Theodore in a regular public school. Under the guidance of their doctors and therapists, they realized they needed to do more to help Theodore improve, so, says James, "the interest in homeschooling started right around that point with the diagnosis and realizing what he's going to need."

So, at that point, Louisa and James started their homeschool journey with Theodore. It was the right decision.

"We were seeing," says James, Theodore "was able to thrive in a setting where he had more freedom than he would be able to get in a traditional school setting." Because of this freedom, "you could see him learning in his own way and it was all happening organically and not sitting at a desk following a curriculum."

Louisa and James decided to homeschool Theodore under a private school affidavit, which in California is a form that declares one's home as a private school. It is the way to homeschool independently, without enrollment or association with an entity such as a homeschool charter school. For Theodore's parents, this avenue seemed best because it gave them "a lot of autonomy in what we were doing with him." "We wanted the most independence we could have," says James.

Independently homeschooling Theodore was a challenge for Louisa and James financially. They were not only paying for education resources for their son, but they were also paying for medical costs such as therapies, some of which were not covered fully by insurance. They had financial problems, but, says James, "that's the choice to be more independent and we were willing to make that sacrifice."

Louisa and James did a great deal of research to find the best curriculum and the best way to homeschool Theodore. "There's a lot of trial and error that has gone on over the years," says Louisa. Some curricula would be successful for a while, but then they would have to switch.

"We evolved over the years into doing a complex combination of curriculum-based learning and child-directed learning," says Louisa.

One of the things that Louisa discovered early on when homeschooling Theodore was that trying to do regular school at home, with a rigid schedule, did not work. "He would shut down," she said, so she loosened up the schedule and he started to thrive.

"Over the years," she says, "we learned that education and learning can happen in a lot of different forms."

Certain subjects fascinate Theodore, "so we will spend months or more going to the library and just getting all the books we can find." Theodore will read the books, ask questions, and there will be discussions and conversations. Louisa describes it as an old style of learning, with reading primary source books and talking over the dinner table. However, this style of learning suits her son better than a traditional boxed curriculum with worksheets and workbooks. "Theodore doesn't thrive as much on them," she says.

On a usual day, Theodore has daily chores. The family has a farm, so he is charged with chores having to do with the animals on the farm. Assuming there are no appointments he has to keep, Louisa says that Theodore "gets to pick what and where he wants to do his work and, if he has a directed project he wants to work on, then we will try and get the necessary things out of the way first and then he could spend the rest of the day working on the things that he wants to really dig into."

"There are other days where we've got music lessons and we've got other therapies and we're out all day with that," she says. When Theodore has a day like that, Louisa says, "I don't push the book work as much because he's pretty tired after that."

In terms of addressing Theodore's specific special needs, Louisa starts by asking, "Is education just sitting down in front of a book and at a desk?" For her son, "education has also been about how to interact with people." What people would consider normal interaction for a child, "we've had to help teach him, so whether it's occupational therapy, speech therapy, or other physical therapies that he's had, we've had to take those at home and incorporate them into our education itself."

Louisa says she looks for "curricula that are going to have some flexibility and that are going to appeal to his interests." "Sparking his interest," she says, "will allow him to focus better on whatever the subject is that we're trying to learn."

She will mix and match subjects, such as science and history, to address Theodore's interests, "so he's excited to do it." It is the principle of "using his strength to then help address some of the weaker areas."

At the time of this writing, Theodore is 13 years old and Louisa and James have homeschooled him for around eight years. "I think we've learned to roll with the punches," says Louisa, "and when something doesn't work, we don't hesitate to find something that does."

Because homeschooling has allowed them to find what works best for Theodore, Louisa says with satisfaction, "he's thrived very well and we've seen huge progress in areas that previously were extremely difficult, particularly writing."

In fact, from not wanting to write at all, Theodore now wants to write books. The day before the interview for this book, Theodore "just finished a short little book that I'm now starting to edit." "This kid," says Louisa with admiration, "is typing out pages and pages and pages of things."

"The expressive language was very challenging for him," says Louisa, "and we're still working on some things, but now he understands how to do it in a way that is quite amazing to see and in a way we couldn't imagine that he would get here."

Theodore himself says, smilingly, "I feel great!" "I feel like I've done a great deal and made progress," he explains, "and learned a lot from books."

Louisa shudders to think of what life would be like for Theodore if he were in a regular public school. "You can imagine him having a temper tantrum in the middle of the class," she says, and other kids would "start taunting him and bullying him because of his behavior and because of those things that they are not suffering from."

When he is having a bad experience, Louisa says that Theodore's "brain shuts off and he can't learn and he can't absorb any information." As a result, "he would be presenting himself as someone with much lower ability than what he really is."

Louisa says that Theodore has taken a few classes outside of their home that are available through homeschool organizations. Overall, these experiences have been very successful. The teachers are private contract teachers and the family has had excellent communications with them, especially when there have been occasional blips. According to Louisa, "they were able to make accommodations and be as positive and encouraging in a way that I know is just not possible in the public schools."

While Theodore has great experiences in the occasional homeschool classes he takes, Louisa says most of his learning is done "quietly at home and that's when he's learning the best."

Louisa acknowledges that "homeschooling isn't the right thing for every family," but "we really clearly believe that this is the right thing for our family." Families must make a commitment since it is a family endeavor, "which is why we love it, because it makes education and learning part of family life."

To those parents who have children with special needs, Louisa has this advice:

> If your child has challenges, it is possible to do homeschooling. In our case, homeschooling is what allowed him to thrive. So it is the opposite of what people say, "Oh, my goodness, how can you do that because it's so difficult or impossible." It's actually what has allowed him to get on the path to be the most that he can be, to be successful, and to walk to the beat of his own drum. Special-needs kids need to find their place and what they're good at. Yes, they have to work on skills that are terribly difficult for them to survive in the world. But when you allow your child to thrive and to feel successful . . . you're able to teach them to fly in a different way.

Theodore sums it up best when he says that everyone has to "find the fun."

CHAPTER FOUR
Homeschooling Unites Parents Across the Political Spectrum

A common myth about homeschooling is that only people with a conservative political viewpoint engage in homeschooling. Because conservatives are less sanguine about the effectiveness of government, including the government-run public schools, many believe that it naturally follows that all homeschool parents must lean to the right.

In a polarizing, but widely reported interview, Harvard University law professor Elizabeth Bartholet claimed, "Over the decades, right-wing Christian conservatives became the dominant group" in homeschooling.[67] It turns out that such claims fail to acknowledge the current state of homeschooling and how homeschooling appeals to a wide cross section of Americans of all political persuasions.

Dr. Brian Ray is head of the Oregon-based National Home Education Research Institute and has studied the homeschool movement for decades. In 2021, he wrote: "A demographically wide variety of people homeschool—these are atheists, Christians, and Mormons; conservatives, libertarians, and liberals; low-, middle-, and high-income families; Black, Hispanic, and white; parents with Ph.D.'s, GEDs, and no high-school diplomas."[68]

Brianne Happel, director of an Oregon homeschool program, says, "There is a substantial and growing population of homeschooling families today, all unique, with vastly different beliefs and reasons for why they homeschool."[69]

Indeed, according to one national homeschooling organization, "homeschooling has continued to grow by leaps and bounds, especially as it has increasingly come to be seen as an acceptable educational alternative." More families "have begun homeschooling for neither pedagogical nor religious reasons but rather for individual pragmatic reasons, including concerns about bullying or the poor quality of local schools." As a result, "This increasing diversity has the potential to change the face of the movement."

That change is currently happening before our eyes. For example, in the wake of the COVID-19 school closures and the often poorly planned distance-learning programs employed by school districts, a large percentage of parents are now considering homeschooling their children.

According to a 2020 RealClear Opinion Research poll, 40 percent of families surveyed said that they are more likely to homeschool their children after the pandemic subsides. Among these parents, 46 percent identified as Democrats versus only 42 percent who identified as Republicans.[70]

In this chapter, you'll learn about how two mothers with very different political viewpoints came together to start a homeschool co-op.

DARCY HOWARD

When asked about where she places herself on the political spectrum, homeschool charter-school teacher Darcy Howard says without hesitation, "Oh gosh, flaming liberal."

Her parents "are both super conservative," but "my brother, sister, and I are all liberal." She grew up in the San Francisco Bay Area in the East Bay town of Pleasanton, went to public school, which she enjoyed, and then went to the University of California at Santa Cruz, "which has always been considered the alternative liberal campus."

"I'm a feminist, I'm pro-choice, I'm pro-gay marriage," she says. "If you pick a liberal issue, I'm on that side of it."

As a liberal living in a conservative area near Sacramento and as someone who is intimately involved in the homeschooling arena, she has been able to see why many people homeschool, and it is most often not about politics.

"Many people think that people homeschool because they don't want their children to get a liberal agenda in public school," she explains, "and there are some people like that, but the majority of people that I know that homeschool do it, not for that reason, but because they want their children to not be limited by the curriculum."

Instead, "They want their children to have the opportunity to learn more than what the state says they have to, and they want their children to learn in whatever manner [that is best for them], not in the method that the state says they should be learning."

"So," she notes, "I would say that's both conservative and liberal [homeschoolers]." And whether people are conservative or liberal, "Most folks want their kids to be fully developed rounded human beings, to have interests, and to have the opportunity to develop themselves to the fullest."

"The first [homeschool] co-op I belonged to," she recalled, "had Mormons, other Christians, Buddhists, and atheists all working together and everybody's bringing something of value." Indeed, "that's one of the things that we all agreed on in our co-op is that we're not about religion, we're about educating our children, and about bringing different viewpoints to our children so that they would become well-rounded young people."

She pointed out that in her county "you get a more conservative homeschooler because it's a conservative community, but you also get a lot of people like me." "I know a lot of people in this area," she emphasizes, "and we're not teaching our kids politics."

Further, she points out that homeschooling is not limited to conservative areas of the state. In liberal coastal Santa Cruz County, "there are a lot of homeschoolers out there and I'm sure some of them are conservatives, but [many] are pretty liberal."

Her own experience with her own two children also demonstrates the diversity of education possibilities and the types of people who take advantage of them. Her kids were in a Montessori charter school, homeschooled, and public high school.

When she first decided to homeschool her oldest child, "I knew nothing about homeschooling." She started off by joining a newly formed homeschool co-op. One good definition of a co-op states:

> A homeschool co-op is a group of families who meet together and work cooperatively to achieve common goals. Co-ops can be organized around academics, social time, the arts, activities, crafts, service work, or projects—or some combination of these.
>
> Activities and classes that are part of a co-op may be led by parents, or the parents may chip in to pay all or some of the teachers and activity leaders. There may be as few as three families in a small co-op or as many as several hundred children in the largest co-ops.
>
> Co-ops may meet in homes, churches, libraries, or community centers. In the United States, homeschool co-ops commonly meet once a week from "after Labor Day" to "before Memorial Day"—but some meet twice monthly or once per month, year-round. A co-op's meeting frequency and yearly calendar is up to the co-op organizers.[1]

In the co-op that she joined, children got together one day a week. Darcy had to teach a class and "everybody taught one class for half a year and then the other half of the year they were off." She recalled that one of the women who started the co-op was a scientist "and she taught really great in-depth science classes." The co-op parents had a wide array of knowledge, from economics to art, "and so they had all this rich experience."

In addition to coming together for instruction, the co-op would have holiday parties, field trips, camping trips, and other group activities. Eventually, she started to homeschool her youngest child as well. The co-op stayed together for five years until it fell apart because the founder, who was the glue of the co-op, sadly passed away.

At the time that the co-op was folding, her youngest child was taking a piano class with the daughter of Sarah Bailey, whose story will be told later in this chapter. Darcy and Sarah met while waiting to pick up their kids from the class.

Bailey is conservative and religious, but she and Howard decided to form another homeschool co-op together. It started off small and met in people's homes. "And it eventually got bigger," says Howard, "and we didn't fit in people's houses anymore, so we had a friend that had a studio that she allowed us to use for the group."

"It was a really good co-op," she says, where parents would teach for a month. So, for example, in U.S. history, one parent would teach for a month and then pass the curriculum to the next parent-teacher.

The co-op was mostly made up of middle-school-aged children and used a hands-on curriculum. So, for science, a murder mystery for the children was created where the kids "had to analyze all the evidence, so that was the science part of it." She makes the interesting observation that while that activity "was super fun and engaging, it's way too much prep work to do with just one or two kids in your house." However, "I'm willing to do it for an entire class."

To Howard, "the benefits of a co-op are interacting with other children, learning from other adults, participating in group activities, where you're not just in an individual learning situation." She told her own children, "You always have to be involved in something that I'm not involved in because it is important to learn from other people and be around other kids."

Also, the co-op would do field trips twice a month. The field trips would get her children "super interested in the topic and then they would want to go home and learn more after they had seen it in person." This use of field trips to spark interest in learning is the opposite of how conventional schools have students first study a topic and "then they go on the field trip as a culminating activity."

Eventually, Howard decided to go back to school to get her teaching credential. Her children then went to public high school. She currently works as a teacher for a homeschool charter school. She meets with parents and their children periodically to advise them and keep students on track. As she explains:

> As a charter-school teacher, you're called a teacher of record, meaning that you're the person who's ensuring that the student is progressing forward in their education and meeting the state standards. I spend a lot of time with families helping them figure out what is their child's learning style; does this curriculum fit them; do we need to try something else? . . . So a lot of my job is helping families figure out what a student's roadblock is and how are we going to get over them. Sometimes it's with the curriculum and sometimes it's me just teaching them something at a meeting briefly that they hadn't thought about such as doing a math problem in a different way, where all of sudden, they say, "Oh, now I get it." So I'm not going in once a month

trying to teach them all their lessons. That's the value of us as credentialed teachers in this space, helping the family create a roadmap for their kids that's going to meet their individual needs.

"I find that my job," she says, is to give parents "permission to think outside the box." "If you grew up in a bricks-and-mortar school, you're trained to only do things one way," she points out, "and it takes a lot of unlearning to get to the point where you're willing and able to think outside the box in terms of education."

Indeed, "A lot of parents think that they're basically going to do public school at home and then they realize that homeschooling offers such a broader richer range of things for them to do."

In the end, Howard says homeschooled children "have such a rich way of thinking about the world because they learned to look at things from a different perspective and really be responsible for their own learning." These students then take what they have learned into the work world and "they're cooperative and they're good problem solvers."

"I think homeschoolers have a great opportunity to really enrich society," she concludes.

SARAH BAILEY

While Darcy Howard proudly proclaims that she is a flaming liberal, Sarah Bailey, who co-founded a homeschool co-op with Darcy, is equally proud to say that she is conservative and Christian.

Although they may seem like a political odd couple, they came together because their focus was on what was best for their children.

As a child, Bailey's school life was not easy. Growing up in Northern California, she attended public schools, but says, "my journey through public school was not pleasant."

"It was back in the 1980s," she says, and she had dyslexia, which was never diagnosed. With sadness, she says, "it was just kind of a shame." Specifically, she recalled:

> I remember being in the fifth grade, I just moved and started in a new school. One of the spelling words on the test was the name of the school, which was Pleasant Grove, and I couldn't spell "pleasant." I remember the parents and teachers that were creating my spelling tests saying, "Even a second grader can spell Pleasant Grove, why can't you?" So that was my first memory as far as really feeling shamed about not being able to spell. My dad suffers from dyslexia as well, so I think my parents believed I would survive. So there was a lot of shame about turning papers in, since this was long before computers and spellcheck. I am a super creative speller and I can spell the same word five different ways in the same paragraph. I had to learn a lot of tricks just to hide that and survive. So, feeling inadequate or stupid most of the time was what I felt like.

By the time she was in high school, she says that she really stopped trying because "I kind of gave up on myself at that point."

After public school, she attended community college in California and then in Utah. But it was when she went on a mission to Poland for her church "where I realized I could do hard things."

She returned from Poland and attended the University of Utah and got a degree in child life therapy. After graduating, she did an internship at a hospital. She had a baby right after her internship, so she decided to stay home. She now has three children.

Bailey, her husband, and their children moved from Utah to California. She says, "we never thought we would homeschool" because "we thought that homeschool kids were weird, and we didn't want our kids being weird."

However, both her sister and her sister-in-law homeschooled their children "and we were surprised by how normal the kids were turning out and how well educated they were." At the same time, she and her husband were getting very frustrated with the public schools their children were attending "and the amount of homework they were being given and the stress and the kind of sexuality that was going on, where my little third grader was talking about everybody pairing up and having boyfriends and girlfriends and we just didn't like where that was going." It was at that time that they pulled their third grader out of school and decided to homeschool "and we never looked back."

She recalled a heartwarming and telling incident that occurred just after she pulled her third-grade daughter out of public school. She and her daughter were walking to school to pick up Sarah's youngest daughter, who was in the first grade and who had not yet been pulled out of school. While they were walking, her older daughter held her hand.

"I said to her that you never hold my hand anymore," Sarah remembered. Her daughter looked up at her and said, "Yeah, I don't care what those kids think anymore." "I felt like I got my daughter, my little girl, back for a couple more years and it was so wonderful," said Sarah.

She had a name for homeschooling: "I always called it boutique schooling. I wanted them to have more of a boutique education where things were customized and designed in a way that I could choose for them what they would thrive in."

At the beginning of her homeschool journey, her homeschool bible was *The Well-Trained Mind: A Guide to Classical Education at Home* by Susan Wise Bauer and Jessie Wise. According to Bauer's website, the book "offers parents a clear, step-by-step guide to providing their children with an academically excellent, comprehensive education, from preschool through high school—one that will teach young students to read, think, and understand, and to be well-rounded and curious about learning." The book also "provides book and curricula recommendations and teaching methods for every grade, in every subject."[72]

"I just devoured that book," says Bailey. Children learn Greek and Latin and read classical literature. "We stopped using textbooks entirely, except for math, which we did online," she recounted.

Much of her children's learning came just from reading: "My children read and read and read and read and I never gave them a spelling test. We never had many grammar lessons, but they learned to spell and write well because they read all the time."

Of course, deciding on the right curriculum for a particular child involves some trial and error. But the great thing about homeschooling, Sarah points out, is "you can change completely."

For example, she used a conventional type of math curriculum for her son, but her son just wasn't getting algebra so she switched to a different math curriculum that people can use when they are running a business or in other real-life situations. "I could totally customize [the curriculum] to fit the needs of each child," she says.

As she homeschooled her children, her thinking and methodology evolved:

> Okay, so the longer I homeschooled, the more organic I got. So, in the beginning, I ran it just like school. I had different periods set up with recess and lunch and everything. And then I said that this is stupid. This doesn't work. So, basically, by the end of my career in homeschooling I would sit down with each child at the beginning of the week, go over their goals, and go over my expectations for them. We would talk about it and then it was up to them to get their work done throughout the week. I never had to check on my girls. They did it all and made it really easy. My son, on the other hand, needed more reminders and few more kicks in the behind to get things done. But at the end, it was really up to them to set their goals and to achieve their goals.

She observes that this self-direction helps homeschooled children later in life. "If you think about it," she says, "when they go to college, nobody's going to be demanding they turn in a paper and their professors don't care if they fail the class." Further, "if you go to a job, if you're not autonomous, you're going to get fired, and you're not going to get your hand held." "So," she believes, "homeschooled kids, when they go to college, and when they get a job, they actually are a lot more prepared in that way because they have self-regulated for so long."

During her time homeschooling, Bailey and Darcy Howard, her flaming liberal fellow homeschooling mom, started up a homeschool co-op together. Sarah described a co-op as a "kind of boutique schooling, where you can get together with a group of parents and the parents can divvy up the different chores or you can hire out."

Originally, the co-op had eight families, but grew over time. At the start it was an all-girls co-op because "we just knew that girls learn differently than boys" and "they had so much fun learning."

"Each parent," explained Bailey, "took a turn and taught something about which they were passionate." Parents taught subjects ranging from history to geography to singing.

"I taught creative writing," said Sarah, which "I know that sounds crazy for me being dyslexic to be a creative writing teacher." However, "I teach it in such a fun way that we just have fun, laugh a lot, and we get up, we move, we dance, we sing, and we use our imaginations and we have a great time." She used a particular curriculum where "I could just put on a show and get children excited [about writing]."

She recalled another liberal friend who had to take her daughter out of public school because of the stress her daughter was experiencing at school. Her friend was very upset about the prospect of having to homeschool her daughter, but after a year of homeschooling her friend said that not only could she do that again, but it was the best time she had ever spent with her daughter.

"People all over the political spectrum have homeschooled for various reasons," she says. "Because when it comes down to it," she emphasizes, "we're all parents and we want to do what's best for our children." So, "there is a market out there for people, who just want a secular education, to homeschool as well."

Eventually, she started the Love of Learning homeschool-learning center.

Love of Learning has two locations in Northern California and is an approved vendor for various homeschool charter schools and receives payments for its classes from parents at these schools (this type of charter school will be discussed in Chapter Six). About 90 percent of the center's funding comes from these charter-school parents.

In describing her center, Bailey says:

> We offer four periods a day, three days a week, but each class is once a week. So you could take two full days from us and you would have eight different classes. Each class is an hour and 10 minutes long. Parents can completely cherry-pick what they want. They can drop their kids off for one class or they could drop them off for three full days if they want. We used to be just three days a week, but we've opened Friday for once-a-month classes. On Fridays, we have woodworking or a cooking class or we now have a service project class. We have those once-a-month classes on Fridays and the once-a-week classes on Tuesday, Wednesday, and Thursday.

Currently, there are about 700 families who are making use of the classes and services provided by her learning center. There are no more than 16 students in any class. Love of Learning does not use textbooks, but instead uses primary sources such as literature. Also, the classes emphasize critical thinking because, as she says, "we don't want to teach children what to think, we want to teach them how to think."

Bailey has seen much in her years homeschooling her own children and then helping so many other homeschooling families. "When I talk to parents about homeschooling," she says, "there's so much fear in stepping outside the box and thinking they're going to close doors for their children."

Parents "are concerned about the end game, whereas teachers are just concerned about getting to the end of the year." The bottom line, Sarah says:

> The love that you have for your child will do wonders and I would just say to parents, don't fear coming home; don't fear doing something different; and don't fear fighting for your child and going down a different path than you know. Most of us were in public schools so we don't know what we don't know. So, educate yourself, learn about what homeschooling is, and take the leap. We're all in the water waiting for you and the water is warm.

CHAPTER FIVE
The Importance of Safety to Parents

There are a wide variety of reasons that motivate parents to choose the homeschool option for their children. Among these, safety has always been one of the top concerns pushing parents into homeschooling.

In its 2020 Schooling in America survey, the school-choice organization EdChoice found that safety remains the top and most important reason why parents choose to homeschool their children:

> … half of parents with homeschooling experience say a safe environment was a high priority for choosing to homeschool. Safety was also the top reason (28%) why parents who prefer homeschooling (regardless of where their children attend school) to other forms of education do so. Black parents (57%) were

more likely than Hispanics (41%) to cite the desire to find a safe learning environment as the reason for homeschooling, but safety remained the top factor regardless of racial background.[73]

Homeschool leaders have for years noted the primacy of safety among the reasons why parents decide to homeschool.

"In public school this is where you see a lot of societal problems with kids . . . (such as) bullying, and discrimination and the violence, frankly," says Rosalynn Newhouse of Oregon's Home Education Network.[74]

The head of Homeschool Louisiana has said that parents were increasingly concerned about "the violence, the bullying, the unsafe environments" in schools.[75]

While bullying may be the most common safety concern among parents, it is important to point out that much more serious incidents happen at schools. To the utter frustration of parents, even when such incidents occur and target their children, schools may not respond appropriately to the seriousness of the incident. That is exactly what happened to the mom profiled in this chapter. The names in this section have been changed to protect the individuals' identities and privacy.

JANE

What happened to Jane's son is shocking. One of her son's classmates allegedly created a "kill list," that included the name of her son. Even after school officials discovered the list, the alleged perpetrator went virtually unpunished, with her son made to feel like he was somehow at fault. No wonder, then, that she and her husband decided to homeschool their son.

Jane and her husband have five children ranging from five to 17.

Her kids are receiving their education in various ways. For example, her oldest child is in a public high school, which has not handled the COVID-19 crisis and the resulting distance learning particularly well. Jane observes that at the school "hours of instruction are completely lacking."

Also, while some teachers have worked very hard, "some of them, they feel like they've just given up on [students]." She notes in exasperation, "it's super unfortunate when you are taking an Advanced Placement class and you feel like your teacher isn't teaching you anything and you have this giant test at the end of the year that you don't feel prepared for."

According to Jane, the problems with her oldest son's school, however, stemmed from the school district. "We didn't feel like [the district] was fighting for the kids," she observed. "They were cowering behind other things," she said, "and the kids never seemed like the most important part of the equation."

Her youngest son is a third grader who loves reading and building things. "He's just a sweetie," she says, and "he's just a little love to his mom."

She has two daughters, a second grader, who had been in public school, and a transitional-kindergartener. She is homeschooling both of them.

But it is Greg, her middle son who is in the eighth grade, who came into homeschooling under the most harrowing of circumstances.

When Greg was in the seventh grade in a public middle school, he experienced every parent's nightmare.

"I was picking up other kids from school," she recalled, "and I got a phone call from a school safety officer at his school." Getting a phone call from the school safety officer almost always brings bad news, but the magnitude of the bad news she received was off the charts.

"He was calling me," she explained, "to tell me that one of the boys in school...had made a kill list and Greg's name was on the kill list."

When the alleged perpetrator was brought in and questioned, he painted himself as a victim and claimed he had been bullied. Rather than try to investigate and find out the real facts, school officials "treated all the kids that were on the kill list as if they were the problem."

"One of my friend's sons," she said, "they actually pulled him into the office that day because he was number one on the kill list and they treated him like he was the problem." Her friend "didn't know that her son had basically been in the office all day and she was livid."

Her friend warned Jane that the school was going to call Greg into the office just like they had done to her son. She, of course, reacted strongly, saying that her son "is not the one who is threatening other students, so what's he done wrong?"

She met with the safety officer and pressed him for details about the incident and why the alleged perpetrator had put Greg on the kill list. The officer replied only with vague generalities about the alleged perpetrator's claim that Greg had supposedly been mean to him. Of course, this response did not sit well with Jane.

She told the officer, "If you think that you're going to pull Greg into the office, I will be there." Further, "I will not let you talk to him without me because he doesn't need to be treated like he was the problem." In the face of her determination, the officer backed down and said that he would not call Greg into the office.

When she talked to Greg later that day, he related how two days before he had dropped his lunch in the school hallway and as he leaned down to pick it up the perpetrator allegedly came by and kneed him in his stomach as hard as he could for no reason.

"So if anyone is a bully, it is the author of the kill list," she says. But, because the alleged perpetrator claimed that the kids on the kill list were somehow mean to him, "all of a sudden he became the protected student and nobody else was validated."

Infuriatingly, the school officer never got to the bottom of any specific instances of what mean things were supposedly done to the alleged perpetrator and what Greg supposedly did to this boy.

She subsequently met with a different safety officer and explained the violence that had been directed at Greg. "You guys need to understand," she emphasized, "these are some of the things that Greg has been dealing with here and you're making him out to be the bad guy and that's just not okay."

Things got worse, however. She said, "what was extra frustrating was that they wanted Greg to do restorative counseling with this boy."

According to one definition: "Restorative justice is seen as an alternative to traditional punishment, which is impersonal, focuses on the offense and placing blame and guilt, and holds attention on rules and processes." Instead, "Practices of restorative justice focus on repairing the harm done by rebuilding the relationship through collaboration and communication."[76]

Greg decided to attend the restorative justice meeting with the alleged perpetrator, even though Jane told him that he did not have to go. The meeting was between Greg, the perpetrator, and a school counselor.

She had told Greg, "You need to let them know that these are the things [the perpetrator] has done to me and it's not okay." Further, Greg needed to make sure "the counselor understands what he is doing to other people and why, because we want this to improve."

At the meeting, Greg told the counselor about being kneed in the stomach. But reported Jane, "he said that he didn't feel like anything happened, that anything changed with this student." At least, however, "He felt that the counselor finally understood [Greg] was not the problem and he walked away thinking, 'Okay, I know I'm not the problem and now she knows I'm not the problem, either.'"

While Greg came away with the relief that the school was not fingering him as the problem, she said that the school did not do anything about the alleged perpetrator:

> They just let it go. They never punished the student. They didn't suspend him. They didn't expel hm. He truly had no consequences for his actions, other than everybody knowing what he'd done. That really frustrated me because their idea was, well, he's already having a hard enough time as it is and so we don't need to add punishment on top of it. And my thing was, but he needs to know what he did was wrong and the only way for to do that is if he had some sort of punishment. But he never got any kind of punishment.

"I told [the school] that I didn't see how you could not punish [the perpetrator]," she said, but "their response was we feel he has already been punished enough because of all the talking he's had to do and now everybody knows what's going on and then we're going to make him do this restorative justice counseling." Her reaction, however, was "I don't think that's good enough."

Jane did talk to some of the other parents whose children had been named on the kill list. She said they "were, of course, furious."

As a result of the school's frustrating and exasperating decision to not do anything significant to punish the student who had allegedly threatened to kill their child, she and her husband discussed their options. Although they were upset about the school's inaction, "we didn't go pitchforks down to the district office if that was going to make things harder for our son."

They thought about other schools in the area, "But we're not really pleased with what the schools are looking like right now, and we don't feel like other middle schools in our area would solve the problem—they have their own problems and we didn't feel like that would be a better solution."

She and her husband ultimately decided to go to home-schooling. And while safety was their top reason for making this move, there was another important and troubling reason they cited.

In some of Greg's classes "there would be a student who had different beliefs or different belief systems and would dominate the classroom." But, she said, "when Greg, who is thoughtful in the things that he thinks and feels, would try to speak up, he would be silenced, or he would be basically told he was a horrible person because he had different beliefs from this person."

"I didn't feel Greg got to be Greg," she said, "because he had to edit himself so much, especially in some of those classes where you want to have a more free discussion in your English class or in your history class, and you want to have discussions about what's going on in the world."

The school's teachers "didn't try to present all sides and they were okay to the one dominant student saying her piece and belittling other kids who said anything against her without any kind of repercussion." So the teachers were "picking a side by default."

She says that she is "super concerned" about the "indoctrination of my children." So, "as much as I actually would like to send my children back to public school, I don't know that I can, in good conscience, do that because of the agendas that are being pushed there."

Even after she started homeschooling Greg, she saw the impact of the school's biased practices.

In one assignment, she asked Greg to write an autobiographical poem. Greg wrote a rough draft, showed it to his mom, who thought it was well done. However, when Greg came back with his final draft and showed it to her, "it was different from his rough draft." He had changed a portion of the poem, where he said he liked to talk about politics. She then asked him why he changed that part of his poem.

Greg said that since the final draft was what he was turning in, he did not think that he should put in that line. She was shocked and said: "Oh, sweetie, you're homeschooling this year. This is your year to be you. You get to write about the things that you want to write about, and I don't want you to censor yourself. I want you to be free." The results were instructive for anyone worried about the impact of classroom in-doctrination on our nation's children:

> And he was, like, really? And I said, "Yes, be you." And so, it's been fun to see. He has had to do a lot of writing this year and he's chosen topics that I know, if he was in a public school situation, he wouldn't have chosen that topic to write about because it could be controversial.

Now, Greg can write and be unafraid in his writing. "I really loved that about him being homeschooled," she says.

Jane is now homeschooling Greg and his younger brother using a charter school homeschool academy (this type of home-schooling will be discussed in greater detail in the next chapter). She says, "they are having a fabulous experience there."

In the end, she says it was "so overwhelming to step into that pool of homeschooling and I always said that I didn't want to do it because it would be a lot of work." "As I've done it," she admits, "I've realized it is even more work than I thought it would be." On the other hand, she says: "Do I feel like my children had a better education this year than they did last year? Absolutely. And so is my work worth it? To me it is."

CHAPTER SIX
Charter Schools and Homeschooling

Many people have the mistaken impression that homeschooling is a very solitary activity. These people imagine a child sitting at the kitchen table with a parent by his or her side. The experience of the parents in the previous chapters demonstrates, however, that this image is a myth. There are various homeschooling options available to parents, from homeschool co-ops to private classes to, in states like California, homeschool charter schools.

According to the National Alliance for Public Charter Schools, "Charter schools are independently-operated public schools that have the freedom to design classrooms that meet their students' needs." Further:

> The reasons that parents choose charter schools for their children are just as unique as the students themselves. They choose char-

ter schools because of the strong, dedicated teachers, because the school's focus matches their child's needs, or simply because their child was struggling in their assigned public school and needed to try something new. Charter schools provide families with options in public education, allowing parents to take a more active role in their child's education.[77]

Homeschool charter schools are a subset of charter schools. There are two main types of homeschool charters. There are charter schools that have a brick-and-mortar facility where classes and services are offered to enrolled children who are being homeschooled. Also, there are non-classroom-based charter schools that have no facility, but offer classes and services through contracted vendors, such as Sarah Bailey's Love of Learning homeschool learning center, which was profiled in Chapter Four.

One of the key advantages for homeschooling parents in enrolling their children in a homeschool charter is that they save money on education costs. One homeschool curriculum company notes that in California, "The state of California pays for the curriculum, supplies, and classes, which works as an advantage for many parents."[78]

This chapter profiles the director of a brick-and-mortar homeschool charter school and a parent at a non-classroom-based homeschool charter.

ALICIA CARTER

One of the top brick-and-mortar homeschool charter schools in California is Natomas Charter School's K-8 Pursuing Academic Choices Together (PACT) Academy. Natomas Charter, located in the Sacramento area, has a number of different academies, ranging from a performing and fine arts academy to a virtual learning academy to the homeschool PACT Academy.

PACT specializes in "assisting families in creating handcrafted, completely individualized education through a family, home, and school partnership."[79] Specifically:

> NCS PACT Academy specializes in helping parents develop an individualized and fully differentiated education for their children. We have teachers specifically trained and experienced in working with gifted and talented students, students with special needs, twice-exceptional students and all kinds of kids who benefit from an experiential, hands-on or non-traditional approach to learning. Our unique model brings students and families to our school site for workshops, parent support, meetings and a huge variety of activities.[80]

When PACT was started in the mid-1990s, "homeschooling charters were in their infancy," observes Academy Coordinator Alicia Carter, "so they were blazing a trail with no precedent since anyone who had homeschooled prior to the charter school movement had done so fully on their own with no guidance and no support." California passed its charter school law in 1992.

Before becoming the head of the PACT Academy, Carter was a teacher at both charter schools and regular public schools. She had also been a consultant for language development for English learners. In 2009, she joined Natomas Charter School as a middle school math teacher. She taught math for six years and then was recruited to be a teacher in the PACT Academy where she taught for five years before becoming PACT's leader.

A mother of three daughters, she originally had placed her oldest daughter in a public school kindergarten, but she told her husband that their daughter, who later would be found to have learning disabilities, "was always going to be a square peg in a round hole and she was always going to function a little differently as a learner than the system we had placed her in." It was then that they switched to homeschooling their daughter. When her two next daughters came along, they, too, were homeschooled. All three have been homeschooled through PACT.

Carter found that homeschooling provided an array of benefits: involving both parents and grandparents in the education of her children; having flexibility with curriculum; promoting stronger bonds between her daughters; and getting her children used to interacting with a wide age range of other people.

One of the important points that Carter makes is that there is a difference between knowledge and credentialism. Opponents of homeschooling will often argue that parents are not qualified or equipped to teach their own children because they do not have the proper training or degree. Carter retorts:

> One of the things that I think we as a civ-
> ilization have lost is the value of knowledge
> in people who don't have the degrees. My
> husband doesn't have a degree. My moth-
> er didn't finish college. But these people
> have these amazing sets of knowledge that
> they're imparting to my children in such valu-
> able ways that are totally legitimate. . . . In
> homeschooling, some knowledge of child de-
> velopment and some knowledge of what kids

should learn is important, but you don't need classroom management skills to manage 30 students. You don't need to learn how to run a parent conference. The learning piece is very often not tied to any sort of formal training. It's just a willingness to share your knowledge. It's one of those things that civilizations around the world value differently than we do in our country.

She points to her father-in-law who "doesn't have the formal paperwork, but the man knows more about earth science and rocks and minerals than anybody I know." "My kids benefit from all of that," she says.

In California, there are two principal ways to homeschool. The first, explains Carter, "is through a private school affidavit, which is where you declare your home a private school, and you are not subject to any regulation by the state, but you do not receive state funding." "You're on your own, go do your thing," she says.

"The other branch of homeschooling is public charter homeschooling," she says, where "you're homeschooling through a public charter school that is sanctioned by the state and a local district and there is access to programs and public education dollars." However, she notes, "with those dollars come oversight and responsibility." "So, basically, if you're homeschooling, you get to decide how much control you want to have and how much resources you want to take advantage of," she says.

Then, within homeschool charters, there is the difference between brick-and-mortar site-based homeschool charters like PACT and non-classroom-based homeschool charters.

All public school students in California, including charter school students, have a certain funding amount tied to them. "At PACT," says Carter, "we put all of our students' money into one pool and then we run a curriculum library, where you check out your curriculum, and a set of classes, where you sign up for what you want to attend." So, she says, the pooled funds "pays for the site where homeschooling families can gather together and support each other and get their children's services."

In contrast, non-classroom-based charter schools have no brick-and-mortar classroom facilities, but they do have credentialed teachers available to support homeschool families. Also, parents at this type of charter school can use the funding tied to their child to purchase curricula and pay for classes at approved vendors such as Sarah Bailey's Love of Learning homeschool learning center.

"So the big difference between PACT and these [non-classroom-based] charter schools is that you actually have some control as a parent about how your money is spent [at the latter]," explains Carter. So, "you'll be assigned a certain dollar amount and out of that dollar amount you purchase your math books, your reading books, your field trips, and your enrichment workshops."

Carter observes that oftentimes families that choose PACT "are new to homeschooling and aren't really sure what they're doing and would like a high degree of support." Additionally, though, PACT gets "people who have been homeschooling for a while, but really want a community to do [homeschooling] together." Children "come here for their classes and it's the same groups of kids that they're seeing, so they build relationships."

PACT also gets reluctant homeschoolers, who fell into homeschooling by accident or because of circumstances. Carter says, "we get a lot of kids who were victims of a bullying situation in school and parents just had to get their kids out and this was all they could figure out to do for a while." So, "it's a temporary thing while they're solving another problem."

Also, citing services such as special education and psychological services, Carter says, "one of the benefits of PACT is that the classes and the services are in-person all at the same place, so you have a single point of contact, and that can be very reassuring for a family who is new to homeschooling or just needs more support."

It is important to point out that parents at PACT still homeschool their children. For instance, PACT offers enrichment workshops to supplement what students are learning at home, ranging from dance to music to drama to art to veterinary science to foreign languages to cooking to poetry writing to physical fitness.

In addition, Carter says, "we have one class where it's just drop in and our math teacher will help your middle schooler with the homework they're stuck on that you can't help them with because you forgot how to do it." Carter smiles and says, "Parents love that one."

Students at PACT are assigned a credentialed teacher who is that student's coach or academic advisor. Students and their parents meet with their teacher every other week to discuss educational needs and progress. Carter says, "at the beginning of term those advisors help you build your workshop schedule and help you make sane choices based on what can your family handle and what is reasonable."

It should be noted that PACT also has a specific program called Project X that does involve classroom instruction in the core subjects:

Project X is a hybrid independent study model that includes two full days of classroom instruction in core subjects. Students then work independently three days of the week. Students have individually differentiated Math instruction, in addition to classes in History, Science, and Language Arts. Students are also enrolled in weekly elective workshops.[81]

One of the big decisions that homeschool parents have to make is what curriculum to choose for their children.

"Sometimes in a family," she observes, "all of the students will use the same curriculum and sometimes we'll recommend different ones based on the kids' needs." So there's guidance, but a lot of flexibility as well.

It is also possible for parents to select a curriculum that is not on PACT's curriculum menu, but that involves a waiver process. She says that the requested curriculum "has to be something secular, no religious materials, and it has to be appropriate to the grade level of the student." Carter, the family, and the family's education advisor will meet and discuss the requested curriculum and "if it's financially and legally an option and a good fit then we order it and sometimes we add it to the selections for everyone." "We try to be really flexible and go with the flow," she says, because "things change really fast."

She clarifies, though, that "if a parent wants to use something on their own and they want to buy it and they want to teach their kids, then more power to you, but it's only when we're paying for it and collecting back the work samples that we have to put it through a screening process and make sure it's appropriate."

One of the things that PACT does well is provide special education services such as speech therapy and psychological services. The school's special education staff members are employees of Natomas Charter School and are located at PACT. In contrast, parents at non-classroom-based homeschool charters can use special education services provided by contracted vendors. She says that both models provide good services, but she says, "it's nice for us that our people work for us and are really focused on our kiddos."

She says, "our special education staff are really good at communicating and meeting with parents in informal ways to help make parents better at making adjustments for their students at home."

Her own daughter has special needs and is a student at PACT. Through the special education staff at the school, she says, "I've learned a lot about my child's learning disability and adjustments I can make and how to make her more successful when we're learning together at home." "I almost never make her sit at the kitchen table and do her work anymore," but rather, "she bounces on a trampoline while she recites math facts and rolls around on the grass." Because she is a homeschooling parent herself, Carter says through her school's specialists "we've learned strategies to help our kids cope."

There are a lot of those special needs "kiddos" at PACT. She estimates that a full quarter of PACT's students have special needs and "that's a really high percentage for a school." "That's what we specialize in," she says, and "we do it well." In fact, when she sees stories in the media saying that homeschooling avoids kids with special needs, she says, "I just start yelling at the TV—give me a call, come see my campus, we do amazing things."

As Carter says, "What's interesting to me is how high the desire is in the parent population for their special education students to do something that is not the traditional [regular public school] program because the traditional program is not working for these kids, and they find real high success here."

As a homeschool parent, teacher, and administrator, she has seen a lot of change in the homeschooling world. Her school had to hold an admission lottery for the first time in its history in 2021. While the COVID-19 pandemic may explain part of that increase in interest, she says, "I think that people are starting to consider homeschooling as a viable option, not a fringe option." Indeed, "homeschooling has become much more diverse religiously, ethnically, and socioeconomically all over this country."

Further, the way homeschooling is being practiced is changing: "Now we're getting a wider variety of people who are just doing things differently or want to do it their own way and less to subscribe to a particular style of homeschooling."

"So I'm excited about our growth and I'm hopeful that the state will value the legitimacy of homeschooling," she says. "I'm a big advocate of school choice and I love that we can do things at a different speed."

HEATHER HARRISON

While Alicia Carter heads up a brick-and-mortar home-school charter school that offers various types of classes on site, Heather Harrison is a homeschool mom whose children are enrolled in a non-classroom-based homeschool charter school, which gives parents the opportunity to pick classes and services offered by a variety of approved private vendors.

Harrison grew up in San Jose, California and still resides there with her family. She attended regular public schools and had a generally positive experience but was also bullied. She was a child development major in college and worked as a nanny.

She and her husband Damien have four daughters ranging in age from six to 21.

She enrolled her oldest daughter in a public elementary school. When her daughter entered first grade, "that's when we really started to notice her struggling." She and her husband wanted to enroll their daughter in summer school, but the school told them that summer session was mainly for English-learner students. They ended up enrolling her in a private afterschool program.

By second grade, her daughter was really having problems with math. She and her husband spent thousands of dollars on tutoring and private programs for their daughter. However, by the third grade, their daughter started to become more aware that she was struggling and not doing as well as her peers.

She says her daughter "was coming home and crying and telling me that she was stupid and that she couldn't do [her schoolwork]."

"I would work with her for hours after school to make sure she got everything done," she recalled, but "at that point we realized something has to change—either she changes schools, or we pull her out of school."

"I realized that if I was coming home and helping my daughter with her homework for four hours without having seen the lessons being taught or how the teacher was executing the lessons then I could certainly homeschool," she observed.

Besides her learning problems, her oldest daughter was also the victim of bullying: "There were other girls at school who were bullying her physically, and not just her but her friends, too." Some of the bullying that her daughter experienced involved physical assaults, "And there was very little that the school did about it," with the perpetrators failing to receive "any real serious disciplinary action against them."

Between her daughter's learning struggles and the bullying, Harrison says, "we knew that we had do something because she could not move on to the fourth grade."

"The only solution [the school] could provide us was to hold her back and repeat the school year," she said, and "I felt that was a non-solution that wasn't going to address what was going on and why she was unable to keep and retain information that she was taught."

"I could see a perfect storm brewing," she said, and "I felt she was going to continue to get further behind and then get bullied by other students and this was going to create a trauma."

She recalls, "It solidified in my mind that the only option for us was to homeschool" because "there wasn't any other place that was going to be able to offer protection from bullies."

Harrison spoke to a friend of hers who had done a great deal of research on homeschooling and had homeschooled her children from the start of their education. She finally decided, "I felt like I could give it a go."

She prepared lesson plans during the summer after her daughter's third-grade year and started homeschooling in the fall.

Using *The Well-Trained Mind* as her guide, she said that the first year of homeschooling "went really well."

For the first initial number of years, she homeschooled her children through a so-called "umbrella school." Also known as a "private school satellite program" in California, an umbrella school provides record keeping and homeschool mentoring and other services to homeschool families.

Thus, for instance, the umbrella school will file the required Private School Affidavit, which independent homeschoolers in California must fill out so that they are viewed as their own private school and will maintain all the records required by the state of California on behalf of the umbrella school's member families.[82]

She joined a twice-a-week homeschool co-op, where her kids took classes and got to socialize, and parents taught classes or volunteered. It was through the co-op that a fellow homeschooling mom told her about the non-classroom-based Ocean Grove homeschool charter school. According to Heather:

> At first, I felt like I didn't want to have strings attached. I wanted to be able to independently homeschool my children and not be told what to do. She explained to me that that's not how Ocean Grove is. They allow you to choose your curriculum and they really just come alongside you and offer things like tutoring and funding. If your child is behind, then you can use funding to help them. Of course, this intrigued me because I really wanted to be able to do that. Also, I wasn't in the best financial position.

At Ocean Grove in 2021-22, family accounts are funded at $3,000 for each high school student, $2,600 for students in grades one to eight, and $2,200 for a student in transitional kindergarten to kindergarten.[83] According to the school:

- The instructional funds (IF) are set up in an IF account that is managed by the education specialist (ES). When families place order requests for curriculum/supplies with an approved product vendor, sign up for classes with an approved service vendor, request online managed licenses (OMLs), or choose to participate in school provided services (ES, High School Support classes, field trips, Science and Art in the Park, etc.) the ES will issue a purchase order from the family's IF account to the approved vendor.

- The state of California funds IEM Charter schools based on average daily student attendance (ADA).

- Instructional fund rates are subject to change each year based on state budget.

- Instructional funding is prorated by day for late enrollment.

- All materials purchased with IFs is the property of the school and must be returned upon leaving our school, including consumables. Parents will be responsible to pay for materials lost, stolen, damaged, or not returned to the school.[84]

The education specialist is a teacher who meets with the homeschooling family regularly and provides "professional consultation in alignment with grade-level standards."[85] As Harrison says, "Their job is to make sure that the students are completing their work and measuring progress."

When their education specialist would have meetings with her and her children, "I bring all their work, [the education specialist] is able to go over it, look at the work, take the physical samples, talk to the children, ask them questions about what they've been learning, and what art projects or things like that that the girls want to show her."

The Harrisons used half the funding for their girls on physical activities. Their middle daughter, for example, is an accomplished ballet dancer, so they spent a chunk of their funding for her on dance classes. Without the funding that came through the charter school they would never have been able to afford such classes.

Her children were able to take a variety of enrichment classes, ranging from art classes to cooking classes to Lego engineering. "It's up to me how I choose to spend my funding," she says.

These enrichment classes are not provided by Ocean Grove but are available from vendors on their approved vendor list. "Vendors can be anybody," she says, such as "art teachers to ballet teachers to saxophone instructors."

"So I chose vendors who were local to me," she says. She would submit a purchase order to her education specialist. it would then go through the process at Ocean Grove, and once approved "then my daughter can take classes provided there's enough funding."

In addition to enrichment classes, she used her funding to buy curriculum and supplies: "So I can get my Saxon math through them, I can get pencil grips, or I have a full-size model of a human body right now." For lower income people, "it provides curriculum and services that would not be otherwise available to them."

Also, the school "did a lot of field trips, everything from aquariums to art museums to a trip to Washington, DC."

She would homeschool her daughters in the core subjects. She says that she would start the morning with math, have a break, then do English language arts, which would range from spelling to writing, and then in the afternoon she would alternate history and science depending on the day.

One of the things about homeschooling that she really likes is playing learning games with her children. "If your child is in a public school," she says, "the teacher simply cannot just sit down and play learning games."

However, when she homeschools her children, she has created something called Fun Friday, where "we just do puzzles, games, and art, and I feel very blessed that I'm able to do that." One of her daughters "loves Legos and things like that and she just wouldn't have the time to do those sorts of things if she was in a public school."

Overall, says Harrison, "I think that what Ocean Grove has done is to maintain my discipline." "I believe that for me," she says, "and not for everybody, I like the fact that someone is making sure that my kids have everything they need and they're doing what they're supposed to." She observes, "That's a medium between completely independent homeschooling and public school and I like that accountability, personally, but not everybody needs that and that's the beauty of homeschool."

Her oldest daughter, the victim of bullying in her public school, graduated from Ocean Grove and is now in college and getting her degree in criminal justice and plans to become a police officer. If she had remained in the regular public school, Harrison says, "she would have continued to struggle, but by creating a different environment [through homeschooling]... I believe that she was in a safer environment to pursue her other talents."

When it comes to homeschooling in general, "I am truly blessed and I will always be grateful that I'm able to do this because my husband and I sacrificed a lot for me to be able to either stay at home or have [flexible] hours where I could continue to do this and he's been super supportive."

"There's no such thing as one size fits all," she notes, "we don't all wear the same shoe size." Rather, "the reason I'm an advocate for homeschooling and homeschool charter school is because it offers a very diverse and enriched environment." In contrast to regular public schools, "I feel that homeschool offers so much more flexibility to meet the needs of the individual."

"Charter schools, in particular, offer choice to lower socioeconomic families, such as my husband and I," she concludes.

CHAPTER SEVEN
Unschooling

Many people believe, incorrectly, that homeschooling means that parents replicate conventional school at their homes, with all the familiar structure of schools, such as packaged curricula, time periods for subject-matter instruction, and parent as teacher/lecturer/fount of knowledge. The reality, however, is much different, with unschooling being at the opposite end of this rigid top-down belief.

Author and unschooling expert, Kerry McDonald says that the essential idea of homeschooling is simple: "give children more control over their lives and their futures by letting them learn instead of making them schooled."[86] She says:

> Most simply, unschooling is the opposite of schooling. It is learning without schooling—including school-at-home. Unschooling rejects the schooling prototype of education and instead values a learning one that looks nothing like school. The unschooling

approach to education is non-coercive, meaning that children are not required or expected to learn things the way they are in compulsory schools or in school-like settings. Like grown-ups, unschooled children have the freedom to say no. Unschooling dismisses the common accouterments of school, including adult-imposed curriculum, grade levels, subject silos, age segregation, lesson plans, rewards and punishments, and arbitrary tests and rankings. Unschooling separates schooling from education.[87]

"Unschooling is simply living, and allowing your children to live, without the specter of conventional school and school-like thinking," says McDonald, and it fuses "living and learning, of seeing them as one and the same."[88]

"There is no one way to be a homeschooler," she says, but, rather, "You will define and practice unschooling in your own way."[89]

McDonald is one of the most interesting education policy analysts in America today. A senior education fellow at the Foundation for Economic Education, she is the author of the acclaimed book *Unschooled: Raising Curious, Well-Educated Children Outside the Conventional Classroom.*

She received a master's degree in education policy from Harvard and then ran her own education and consulting business.

The mother of four, she became increasingly interested in early childhood education policy when her children were little and "decided to move outside of consulting and back into policy again and that is where I've been for the last 18 years."

A key characteristic of regular schooling, says McDonald, is that it is a top-down process, which "focuses on obedience, compliance, conformity, regurgitation of facts and information, and standardization." She observes that these are all qualities that robots exhibit.

"What differentiates humans from robots," she says, "are qualities like creativity, originality, curiosity, ingenuity, and an entrepreneurial spirit, and yet those qualities are often crushed through schooling methods."

Unschooling, she explains, "really tries to encourage a child's natural curiosity and creativity by allowing them a lot of freedom in what they learn and how they learn and the pace at which they learn, as opposed to following a strict standardized curriculum that's sorted by grade level and subject area and so on."

McDonald says she unschooled her own children because "I think it's really important to encourage young people to have personal agency to be critical thinkers and to be problem solvers and to question and those are qualities that are often stifled in a conventional classroom."

Her children have never attended a conventional school. Living in Cambridge, Massachusetts, she says that the area has so many homeschooling resources, from museums to libraries to bookstores to classes for homeschoolers, plus it has a really diverse homeschooling community.

She believed that if she sent her children to a conventional school, their learning would be limited because "they would go from having this wide variety of experiences, and really being immersed in the people, places, and things of our community, to going to the same stand-alone building every day with the same age-segregated group of kids and the same static handful of teachers."

"I wanted them to have a much broader educational experience," she says.

When her oldest daughter Molly was kindergarten age, McDonald went through the process of researching curricula that she would use to instruct her. She had decided on a particular curriculum, but then was stunned when Molly taught herself to read on her own.

Through the things in her environment, she was also learning about a wide range of subjects, from biology to astronomy. Based on these observations of her daughter, she wondered why a top-down school-like curriculum was necessary when a natural learning process was taking place.

As an example of the self-directed nature of unschooling, McDonald points to Molly's interest in martial arts. Because of this natural interest, Molly started taking classes at a local martial arts studio that had just opened. Her daughter fell in love with martial arts and from that experience she became very interested in Korean language and culture.

They found some free or low-cost online language classes and history classes, which her daughter ended up taking. McDonald then found a native Korean speaker who tutored her daughter three times a week. According to McDonald, her daughter "is well on her way to being fluent in Korean and wants to visit South Korea someday and maybe live there for a semester."

"But that just shows that she was really driving that process," which is an essential element of unschooling. "As a parent," she says, "I was the one connecting her to available resources."

As she says in her book *Unschooling*, "To make the leap to unschooling, I needed to stop thinking of myself as my children's teacher and instead become their follower."[90]

"As Molly's Korean language learning shows," says McDonald, "unschooling doesn't mean that young people never learn 'school-ish' subjects or never take formal classes." She observes, "A great many do!" and that "simply means that they choose to do it, or not."[91]

Unschooling is therefore not some form of educational anarchy but is education that is self-directed by the learner based on his or her interests and passions. The family profiled in the following section epitomize the unschooling experience.

RACHEL CHANEY AND HER CHILDREN JUSTIN AND REBECCA

It is a long way from Santa Barbara, California to Oxford, England, but that is the journey Rachel Chaney has made. It is also a long way from attending conventional schools growing up to unschooling her children in a foreign country.

As a small child growing up in Carpinteria, a small town near Santa Barbara, she was very shy: "I was extremely shy when I was little, like the shyest person you can ever imagine."

Instead of a big public school, her mother chose a very small private school, which Chaney attended through the twelfth grade. She enjoyed the individualized instruction. For instance, because she was academically advanced and she already knew what was going to be taught in kindergarten, the school made a separate curriculum for her in areas such as writing and math. "And that continued all the way through high school," she says, "so it was a pretty positive school experience in that sense."

Growing up, her good friend who lived across the street from her was being homeschooled. Even back then, Chaney says that she "loved that they homeschooled." "They had a kind of closeness as a family," she remembers, and she liked that "they spent so much time together."

After high school, she attended Stanford University, where she received her bachelors and master's degrees. She worked as a teacher at an inner-city charter school in East Oakland. She also worked for a time as a policy researcher at the Pacific Research Institute.

It was through her interest in history that she started to contemplate homeschooling. "I've always loved history, which is what I ended up studying in school," she says, "and, historically, homeschooling was the norm across basically everywhere."

"It's been a relatively recent Western phenomenon to have school be the norm," she relates, "and even once it became the norm in the West [schooling] was for much shorter time, so kids would go for a couple months out of the year, for a couple hours a day." "They spent most of their time learning with their families," she says, "and I loved reading about that and learning about that."

After she finished her degree work at Stanford, Rachel got married. Her husband Eric would go on to become a top expert on the economic history of the Middle East. They have three children, Justin, Rebecca, and Katie.

"Justin is 12 and he's always been very interested in public transportation," says Rachel, "so he likes trains and buses and planes and things like that." "His brain is very unique," she says, "so he reads at an adult level."

Justin is particularly interested post-World War One European history. "So right now, he's reading *The Gulag Archipelago* by Alexander Solzhenitsyn," she says. For anyone who has ever picked up *The Gulag Archipelago*, which is a great, yet dense and thick book, the fact that a 12-year-old is reading it is amazing.

"It's very fun to be his parent," says Rachel with a smile.

Her daughter Rebecca, who is eight, is very artistic and musical. "She's only played the piano for about two years, but she's very gifted musically, which she gets from Eric, not me," laughs Rachel.

Rebecca herself says, "I like to play the piano and I like to sing," and she especially favors "happy classical, and I don't like slow music very much." She laughs saying she likes her music to be "peppy."

Katie is one and a half "and she is a crazy toddler who delights us all," says Rachel.

Justin and Rebecca have never attended a conventional school and have always been homeschooled. Chaney and her husband believe that homeschooling allows for individualized education for each child and keeps a family focus of the world when the children are growing up.

Also, she says that homeschooling fits the needs of their children. For example, in describing Justin, she says, "You could tell his personality, almost from day one, he was very intense, very smart, and very much an introvert, and you could tell— I'm not kidding—from almost the second he was born."

"So, while he enjoys social interactions in small chunks," she says, "I think Justin would be exhausted by having to navigate with dozens of other kids constantly."

Also, "cognitively, I think it would have been hard to find a good fit for him, given that *The Gulag Archipelago* isn't standard reading material for sixth graders."

For someone like Justin, "if we hadn't been homeschooling and he had been in a system where he had to read what the teacher said needed to be read at the same time as all the other kids were reading it, I don't know what would have happened." "I don't think that he would have fallen in love with reading in the same way," she says, where today "I have to pry him away from his book." She estimates that Justin's bookshelves have "30,000 to 40,000 pages of adult non-fiction modern European history that he's read."

Justin himself says, "I'm interested in the lead up to the Second World War, the rise of fascism after the end of World War One, and the Cold War."

Speaking of *The Gulag Archipelago*, Justin says, "I'm reading that book because forms of government interest me and it shows that communism is definitely not the best form of government." "In the Soviet Union, people were put in prison completely arbitrarily and others were political enemies," he says.

"I don't think I would like regular school," says Justin, "because I read things different than what most people my age would read, and [regular schools] assign reading material to you and you need to read that." "I don't want to read a book about superheroes," he emphasizes, "I want to read a book about the Soviet gulag, and if I had to read a book about superheroes I don't think I would like reading."

When they decided to homeschool their children, Rachel and Eric also decided that they would unschool them.

"Unschooling," she says, "is basically requiring your kids to do as little as you as parents feel comfortable requiring so they can have as much time as possible to pursue their own interests." The idea is that "children will learn better when they love something and they will learn better when they are self-motivated to learn it rather than being coerced into learning it by someone else."

Further, she says, "the only learning that really sticks is learning that is motivated by the desire-to-learn model of learning."

Children also need to be respected. She says, "children are people rather than accessories to us adults and so they should be respected as such, even when they are young."

Her own particular way of unschooling her children is actually a bit of a hybrid. She uses a combination of unschooling elements with a little conventional homeschooling.

"I do agree that children are unique individuals and come to us as people who deserve respect and should not be coerced or treated harshly," she says, "and I also believe that learning will only really last if it comes from love and desire to learn." "But that having been said," she also says, "I do believe that it's our responsibility as parents to give our kids the tools they need to succeed in the world and to flourish as happy healthy adults and part of that is to make sure they have a basic set of tools."

"So, if they want to learn something when they are older, they will not be limited by what they were not taught as kids," she says. "For me," she explains, "that means that in their elementary years until they're about 13 or 14, in addition to the ample time we allow them to do what they want to do and pursue their own interests, we require that they learn to read, learn to write, learn to touch type, and also continue basic foundations in math."

In addition to the basic three Rs, she says, "we also really cultivate an atmosphere of learning as a family." She and her children will learn together around a theme that they all choose. They then structure it around a different country every month.

"I had started to try and figure out a systematic way to organize our learning each month," she says. Focusing on something in history led to the children wanting to learn more about where something took place, which then evolved into learning about a different country, a different way of life, and a different government system. Before the school year, they brainstorm a list of countries that they will study.

"We actually make our own curriculum for the countries we study," she points out, which is "separated into a set of resources each month." She chooses read-alouds, which are books like historical fiction or well-written non-fiction that make a particular time or place come alive. She and the children choose two or three of these read-aloud books each month and read them.

Besides studying the country together by reading books about it, they also learn about it by going to museums and other places that help them learn about that country. They will eat food from that country, do crafts associated with that country, study pieces of art from the country, and watch documentaries. "We do that each month," she says, "and it's very flexible and fluid, but it's how we structure our learning time together."

At the end of each month, Rachel says, "we have a big feast of food from that country, where we read poetry from that country, and we call it our poetry tea time."

Although studying countries has structure to it, she classifies it as unschooling "in the sense that it was really initiated by [her children], directed by them, and based on what they're interested in." "A lot of unschoolers still add some structure and expose their kids to some sort of methodology," she notes, "so, I would say it's unschooling."

Overall, she says that her children spend between 30 minutes to an hour on structured activities that they're required to do and which they may not be excited to do. "Usually, they're very open to do it," but she says, "sometimes I have to say, 'No, you really do need to do your math today.'"

So, Rebecca might work on her multiplication tables at the same time that Justin is learning to touch-type on the computer. Rebecca might do some creative writing, while Justin might do a Khan Academy online class on grammar.

"We haven't needed a curriculum that really needs to drill things into them," says Chaney, "and they just basically do a page a day [from a math workbook series] and that's enough to solidify it." For Justin, who is now getting older and has started to do more rigorous math, lessons from the online Khan Academy will supplement the workbooks.

Beyond the required structured activities, she says, "there's probably another hour or so each day that we're learning together, either through me reading aloud or us doing some craft together or whatever."

"The rest of the day," she says, "is spending time with friends or being outside or reading or for playing the piano or drawing and things like that."

Because Chaney does not do a lot of formal schooling, she does have her kids do various jobs because "we find it really important to instill a work ethic in our kids through other things." "The learning stays a fun, curious, and enjoyable thing," she says, while "work is learned through a set of jobs each day," including short household jobs such as cleaning up rooms.

Under her unschooling hybrid, she says, "the kids can study what they love, and they love learning." "They're curious and they're delightful kids who are fun to be around," she beams.

She admits, "like all homeschool moms I am always battling the sense of worry or guilt that I'm not doing enough and that we should be learning this, or we should be learning that, which is a staple of the homeschool experience." "You always feel like you aren't giving enough to your precious kiddos," she says.

When it comes to socialization, she says that her children receive socialization in a much richer way than if they were in a conventional school.

"They're certainly not socialized in the sense that they don't interact with a group of age-restricted peers for eight hours a day," she observes, "but they interact with people of all ages, all walks of life, children of all ages."

According to Chaney, home-education moms will set up classes or group meet-ups and will advertise them to groups on social media platforms "and if your child is interested in something related to what they set up, then you go and meet other people there."

Rebecca met one of her first friends in England at a rock-climbing class. The mother of this new friend invited Rebecca and Rachel to a home-education group that met at a museum, which hosted home-education classes. Through those classes, Rebecca made other friends. "So, it's sort of like a chain reaction and that's pretty common," Chaney says.

Chaney started unschooling Justin and Rebecca while the family was still living in the United States in Massachusetts. Although they now live in England, it turns out that the unschooling experience has not been much different despite the change in country and culture. "The experience is remarkably similar in both places," she says.

"There's a very strong homeschooling community here, where it's called home education more than homeschooling," she says. She has found large supportive communities of homeschoolers in both countries.

The home-education experience in England has been a very happy one for Chaney and her family. "I'm so lucky to have a wonderful group of home-education moms here in England . . . and the kids have just a fantastic group of friends," she says. "Eric and I are always talking about just what lovely, lovely friends [Justin and Rebecca have]," she says, and "the kids here are just so, so nice and very welcoming."

"When the pandemic isn't happening," she reports, "there are lots of homeschool classes, nature groups, choir, and play groups where you just meet all together." "You can really do as much or as little as you want, so if you wanted, you could spend hours each day in some sort of organized class setting, but if you don't want to, you obviously don't have to," she observes.

When asked about her advice to parents who are considering homeschooling, Chaney says, "My best advice is that they should do it."

"Homeschooling is incredibly rewarding, and while it's definitely a time commitment on the part of parents, it's less intimidating than it might seem," she says. As a former teacher herself, she emphasizes, "You do not need teaching experience and you do not need to be an educator by background because each parent knows their child the best and is most equipped to educate their child." Indeed, "because you love your child, you are well equipped to educate them."

Love, in fact, is an integral part of the homeschooling secret. "You're motivated, because you love them, to figure out what works best for them," she says.

CHAPTER EIGHT
Flexibility and the Need for Choice

It will surprise many people that some well-known celebrities have homeschooled their children. Actors, athletes, and other famous folk have benefited from homeschooling. One important reason that these celebrities have opted to homeschool is because of the time and schedule flexibility it offers.

Take, for example, Kris Jenner, star of *Keeping Up with the Kardashians*. Jenner's daughters Kylie and Kendall were having problems balancing a regular school schedule and their careers.

"They were performing poorly in school due to constantly missing classes as the regular 8 AM-4 PM school day clashed with their budding careers," said Jenner. "The girls," she explained, "also weren't able to fully be creative in the typical school setting."[92]

Jenner decided to homeschool through the Novel Education Group, which is "an academic enrichment agency that provides efficient, flexible, customizable homeschooling and private tutoring for K-12 students." Novel says, "Our U.S. accredited courses are available anywhere in the world, empowering K-12 students to tailor their schooling experience to fit their individual goals." Students have the option to "enroll in full-time homeschool programs, pursue highly specialized interests, and complete one-on-one enrichment programs."[93]

Novel specializes in assisting students who have "work, travel, or various other scheduling conflicts." Jenner said that Novel's course offerings allowed her daughters to "create a schedule that fit their busy lifestyles." The homeschool agency allowed them to get their education "and build a successful career at the same time."[94]

Of course, as many people know, Kendall and Kylie would gain great success in modeling and business. And it was withdrawing from regular school and receiving homeschooling that, says Kris, "transformed" their lives.[95]

Many other less famous families have chosen homeschooling for exactly the same reason that spurred Kris Jenner. Here is the story of one mom whose daughter was a budding gymnastics star who needed that flexibility to pursue her passion.

TAMMY SCHER

Born in New York City, Tammy Scher moved to the Los Angeles area before she entered high school. Because of family issues, "I got emancipated by the courts and I was actually homeless for about three months" and "couch-surfing, going around, and then sleeping on the roof of an apartment building."

She worked at a bed and bath store in order to save up money to afford her own apartment. Adversity, however, pushed her to work hard and succeed.

Eventually, she became the owner of Forgotten Treasurez, which is an online wholesaler of fine art. The business took off immediately and 20 years later is incredibly successful.

She has also been the president of her local chamber of commerce in Sherman Oaks, California.

Scher has one daughter, Brooke. "She was a very easy child from a young age," she recalled, and "even before she could walk, she was always dancing, dancing, dancing, loving music and dancing."

Scher put her daughter into dance classes and gymnastics classes. "There was coach at the gym who was a former Olympian, Betty Okino," she said, "and when Brooke was five years old, she told me that Brooke has a talent for gymnastics."

Okino was part of the famed 1992 U.S. women's gymnastics team at the Barcelona Olympics, which won the bronze medal.

Thus, Okino's opinion about Scher's daughter carried weight.

Okino believed that if Scher gave her daughter private lessons "she could really excel." "I thought, well, this is just how they sell their private lessons to people," she said, "but then I found out that nobody else had been asked, just my daughter." "So," she said, "I gave her private lessons, and she did quickly excel."

At six years old, Brooke became the youngest member of the gymnastics team at the gymnastics academy at which she was training. At seven, she started competing "and she even won first place at sectionals when she was eight."

Brooke loved gymnastics and being part of the gymnastics team. She "loved being the little mascot for the team" and she was hanging out with her teammates "nonstop." "She was very social," says Scher.

While her daughter was doing great in gymnastics, her school life was a different story.

Because of her rigorous gymnastics training schedule that would go from 4 PM to 9 PM three days a week and until 10 PM two days a week, Brooke was very fatigued.

"She just wanted to sleep in every morning," recalled Scher, and "it was very difficult to wake her up." She realized that this situation could not continue so when her daughter was in the middle of the first grade, she pulled her out of school to homeschool her.

Scher says Brooke's teacher "was very helpful and said that I could borrow the books that they were using to keep on for the year . . . so I did have some help from the school and the teachers."

There was also a local store that had a lot of supplies and resources for homeschoolers. She "bought all the workbooks that were first grade that I felt were needed—grammar, spelling, math, and social studies—whatever there was, and I would use the workbooks all the time."

Because her daughter did not have to adhere to a rigid school schedule, Scher says, "I would wake her up at 10 AM and we would start homeschooling." Also, rather than covering all subjects every day, "we would do usually two subjects a day and switch out here and there."

Also, she could cover subjects like history in greater depth and teach Brooke why things happened, with less emphasis on knowing "the name of every general and things like that because we all don't remember that stuff unless you're a Jeopardy person." "So," she noted, "I didn't go into those kinds of things that the school would do."

Initially, she homeschooled Brooke independently. In the fourth grade, she enrolled her in a homeschool charter school. Through the charter school she was able to get curriculum, plus "we would do group projects once a month where the kids would get together." "If I didn't like anything," she said, "I supplemented it myself."

A teacher would come to her house once a month "just to check on the progress and everything that we're doing." "So it was a great program I joined," she says.

Because of the flexible schedule, Scher could schedule private gymnastics lessons at 2 PM or 3 PM for her daughter right before her gymnastics class and training. These lessons were taught by the former Olympian Okino. As she says, "we had the advantage that we could come at two o'clock when other kids couldn't come."

Although Brooke excelled at gymnastics, sadly, she developed tendonitis in her shoulder that did not heal. Her daughter, therefore, had to quit gymnastics and Tammy decided to stop homeschooling her.

Scher enrolled Brooke, who was in the eighth grade, in a performing arts public magnet school. This development, however, was not the end of Tammy's school-choice journey. There was one more interesting twist in that road.

With the help and encouragement of the principal at her daughter's school, Scher helped found the Champs Charter High School of the Arts in Sherman Oaks in the Los Angeles area.

Many of the students came from the performing arts middle school that Tammy's daughter had attended. Brooke was one of the students in the new entering class at Champs.

After graduating from Champs, Brooke went on to the University of California at Santa Barbara.

Homeschooling was "very important, very important, because I can't see another [learning situation] that would have worked for the hours that we needed." Without the flexibility of time and scheduling that homeschooling offered, Scher doubts that her daughter would have been able to continue doing gymnastics, despite her obvious talent for it. "She would just not be on the [gymnastics] team," says Tammy, which would have been sad and tragic, since "that was her whole social identity."

Looking back on Brooke's education, Scher has become a strong advocate for parental choice. "It's so important," she says, that education be tailored to the child "because each child is so different in their needs and wants."

CHAPTER NINE
The Post-Pandemic Future of Homeschooling in America

The current state of homeschooling appears to be very positive. The number of homeschoolers across the country is way up and likely will continue to rise in the aftermath of the COVID-19 pandemic.

Further, dramatic improvements in technology plus the huge expansion of learning resources have made homeschooling more accessible for people. The continued missteps and failings of public schools have caused many parents, who would ordinarily send their children to conventional schools, to consider homeschooling.

Finally, with more Americans being able to work remotely from home with flexible work schedules, it is now more doable for many families to homeschool their children. The rise of new learning arrangements among groups of homeschoolers has also made it easier to educate children at home and ensure positive socialization.

The result is a homeschool population that busts the myths about who homeschools, why they homeschool, and how they homeschool. From Tijuana-born homeschool advocate Magda Gomez to "flaming liberal" Darcy Howard to unschooler Rachel Chaney, the parents profiled in this book tear down the stereotypes that have persisted about homeschooling. Indeed, as this book has shown, the diversity of homeschooling is truly eye opening.

Homeschool parents come from different racial, income, religious, and political backgrounds. Their children range from those with special needs to those who are academically advanced. They have decided to homeschool their children for many different reasons, from concerns about the safety of their children to the need for flexible schedules to worry about classroom biases to rebellion against the one-size-fits-all model of the regular public schools.

Mike Donnelly, senior counsel for the Homeschool Legal Defense Association, which is the world's largest homeschool organization and the country's top homeschool advocacy organization, observes: "I have seen homeschooling bridge gaps that people would think are unbridgeable and it's because, as parents who homeschool, we value, number one, parental choice in education." Adherence to that basic principle "cuts across all beliefs, cultures, and political views."

"Parents are the ones who should be making the choices about how their kids are educated," he says.

It is this core basic principle which is the source of the conflict in education debates in America: "That's the big fight right now—who should be making the primary decisions about education in the lives of children and whether the state and government should be the primary socializing force in society."

"In my experience of traveling around the world and advocating for homeschooling, that's the question—who decides?," he asks. "Is the parent the primary decision-maker or is the state the primary decision-maker?," says Donnelly, "and that is a worldview question."

"You can have a worldview as a Christian and a worldview as an atheist and still think that the state should have nothing to do with the education of children," observes Donnelly, "and that's a very powerful shared value." "I think that can bring people together and I have seen it in every country that I've been to," he says.

"There is a tiny number of people," he observes, "who are serious critics of homeschooling and they are statists who believe that the state, the government, should be the primary socializing force in society." "They don't want pluralism," he says, "they want civic uniformity."

Kerry McDonald, the unschooling expert, observes that in addition to the pandemic-caused school closures, parents are "frustrated by what they see happening in terms of the curriculum in schools, both public and private, which is pushing more families into homeschooling."

Rachel Chaney, the unschooling mom in England, says that the view of the government and the public school system that "we know what's best for your children is so damaging to so many children, particularly those who don't fit the standard schooling system, but then would be forced into it."

Fortunately, just when dissatisfaction with the regular public school system is boiling over, the ability of homeschooling to address parent concerns has never been greater.

"I think we're at a real moment of education transformation," says McDonald, "driven by disruptive innovation in education, including learning pods and micro-school networks, facilitated by ed tech, and visionary parents and educators who are building new models or building upon old ones to create better learning methods for the 21st century."

Indeed, the parents profiled in this book have used the wide array of tools now available to help them and others homeschool their children successfully. From Heather Harrison using a homeschool charter school to Carrie Carlson using audio books for her special-needs son to the homeschool co-op formed by Darcy Howard and Sarah Bailey to Demetria Zinga's use of varied forms of social media to advise other homeschooling families, these parents highlight why homeschooling is spreading and becoming so popular.

But, as has happens all too often, where innovative alternatives to the regular public-school system have produced success, defenders of the public-school status quo react by trying to destroy those options. This is certainly the case with homeschooling.

The most highly publicized recent attack against homeschooling has come from Harvard University law professor Elizabeth Bartholet, who has called for a general presumption against homeschooling, with the burden on parents to justify exceptions:

> The new regime should deny the right to homeschool, subject to carefully delineated exceptions for situations in which homeschooling

is needed and appropriate. Parents should have a significant burden of justification for a requested exception. There is no other way to ensure that children receive an education or protection against maltreatment at all comparable to that provided to public school children.[96]

Available research undercuts her claim:

A 2018 analysis by the National Home Education Research Institute (NHERI) of federal and other data on abuse of children found that based on available empirical evidence "the rate of abuse of children in homeschool families is lower than in the general public."[97]

"This shouldn't be surprising," says Kerry McDonald, "as homeschooling parents are often choosing homeschooling while making significant personal sacrifices, to ensure their child's safety and well-being,"[98]

Not only is there "no evidence that [abuse of children] is higher in homeschool families," the analysis found that schools, far from being havens for abused children, are all too often the centers of such abuse:

> Based on empirical evidence to date, there is a remarkable rate of abuse of U.S. schoolchildren by school personnel (e.g., teachers, coaches, bus drivers, administrator, custodians). The multiple laws, regulations, and policies related to public and private schools result in a very small fraction of abuse incidents by school personnel ever being reported to law enforcement or child welfare personnel.[99]

The abuse at public schools, however, goes beyond just school personnel. General crime, bullying and other negative social interactions at public schools occur at shockingly high rates.

In 2017-18, according to the latest available federal data, an astounding 1.44 million crimes recorded by the nation's public schools, including a whopping 962,000 violent incidents.[100] And appallingly, only a small fraction of these crimes and violent incidents are reported to the police.[101]

It is important to understand the breadth of these statistics. Crime and violent incidents are not only happening at a sliver of America's public schools, but at the overwhelming majority. In 2017-18, 80 percent of the nation's public schools reported criminal incidents and 71 percent had violent incidents.[102]

USA Today reported in 2019 that, according to the U.S. Department of Health and Human Services, "about 49 percent of children in grades four to 12 reported being bullied by other students at least once a month and 31 percent of children reported being the ones who bullied." The publication concluded, "Those numbers suggest that it's more likely than not that your child will either be the target of bullying or the instigator."[103]

Jane's son Greg was not a target of bullying, but of a very serious contemplated crime, yet his public school did nothing to protect him from this targeting. Why, therefore, should parents like Jane, who are homeschooling for safety reasons, be forced to send their children back to the same public schools that failed to protect their children in the first place?

Even those few parents given government-sanctioned exceptions to homeschool would still be required by Bartholet to have their children attend mandated "civics education" courses so that those children are exposed to "alternative views and values" propagated at the government public schools. [104]

Bartholet has urged President Joe Biden to clamp down on homeschooling, saying, "If the Biden administration is truly committed to educational reform in our nation's schools, it should do something to address the needs of children kept out of schools entirely by parents who may have no commitment or ability to provide even the basics of an education."[105]

It is not just influential academics like Bartholet, however, that are attacking the growing homeschool movement in America. The teachers' unions, the 800-pound gorilla of education, are also placing homeschoolers in their political crosshairs.

"Teachers' union honchos don't like homeschoolers for obvious reasons," says former Los Angeles teacher Larry Sand, who is head of the National Teachers Empowerment Network. "When kids learn at home, it means less control, money, and power for them," says Sand, which is why the National Education Association regularly adopts anti-homeschool resolutions at its conventions.[106] One adopted resolution stated:

> The National Education Association believes that home schooling programs based on parental choice cannot provide the student with a comprehensive education experience. When home schooling occurs, students enrolled must meet all state curricular requirements, including the taking and passing of assessments to ensure adequate academic progress. Home schooling should be limited to the children of the immediate family, with all expenses being borne by the parents/guardians. Instruction should be by persons who are licensed by the appropriate state education licensure agency, and a curriculum approved by the state department of education should be used.[107]

In other words, according to the NEA, homeschooling should not be allowed, but if it does occur then it should look exactly like the regular public school.

Rachel Chaney observes, "people who want to stay in power don't like homeschoolers because they see them as a threat to their power and that's true, of course, for the teachers' unions and the educational establishment."

The NEA is now worried about the innovative alternatives to regular public schools that have arisen in the wake of the COVID-19 pandemic.

For example, the NEA is going after microschools, which *The Wall Street Journal* describes as "Midway between homeschool and private school," where small groups of students meet at a private residence and instruction is provided by a private education service provider. The union has issued an opposition report on microschools that worries about "widespread support for microschools."[108]

The worry for homeschoolers, of course, is that this type of anti-homeschool pressure from influential academics like Bartholet and powerful special-interest groups like the teachers' unions will cause lawmakers and government officials to either ban or greatly regulate homeschooling.

While some states only lightly regulate homeschooling, others such as New York, impose burdensome regulations on homeschoolers. According to the *New York Post*, New York requires homeschoolers to jump through many hoops:

> On top of a letter of intent [to homeschool], which is due annually, parents need to submit an Individualized Home Instruction Plan (their full education curriculum including syl-

labi, materials and textbooks) followed by four quarterly reports and a year-end assessment. Seven different documents in all, which are due again the following year.[109]

With the increase in homeschooling during the COVID-19 pandemic, some states have tightened the screws on homeschoolers in other ways.

In California, the 2020-21 budget signed by Governor Gavin Newsom froze funding at the 2019-20 level for non-classroom-based charter schools, which include many homeschool charter schools of the type that Heather Harrison's children attend, as described in Chapter Six.[110] Funding was frozen even though the pandemic greatly increased demand for education options such as homeschool charter schools. This funding freeze was also clearly discriminatory because funding for regular public schools was increased.

Harrison says, "Here in California, I feel like we're just fighting for our lives to be able to have non-brick-and-mortar, non-classroom-based charter schools." "My hope is that we can get some laws passed that will keep freedom of education, freedom of choice, so that we stop having to fight every month a new bill or a new this or that put out by the teachers union."

Alicia Carter, the homeschool charter school leader, says: "during the pandemic shutdowns, we shined a spotlight on alternative education, particularly charter schools, and especially homeschooling charter schools, and when you shine a light on something that's doing things differently, then people in the status quo say, 'Oh, look at that thing that they're doing differently.'" The defenders of the status quo then either say, "let's let them be or they say we must kill it."

Carter believes that homeschool charter schools "are taking death by a thousand paper cuts" and California policymakers "are just going to tighten restrictions, increase auditing, and reduce funding." "

"Yeah, it's money and it's control," says Carter, and she is right. Thus, as an alternative to regular public schools becomes larger and more successful, then it becomes a target for the those whose money and control are threatened by the growth of such an alternative.

So in the face of this backlash by the defenders of the status quo, what should homeschoolers and supporters of parental choice do?

Rolling back stifling homeschool regulations should be one priority. "You can't overregulate," says liberal homeschooler Darcy Howard, because "you're going to kill what's special about it."

Also, Kerry McDonald recommends that funding should follow the child. She says, "if education funding supported students rather than school bureaucracies, more families would get access to an array of education options—including these new models [of home-based education] and ones that have yet to be invented."

She points out, "Taxpayers spend about $700 billion each year on U.S. K-12 education." "If that money," she observes, "was redistributed to families in the form of education savings accounts (ESAs), vouchers, tax-credit scholarship programs, and other education choice mechanisms, parents would have more options beyond an assigned district school."[111]

For example, according to the school-choice organization Ed-Choice, Florida's Family Empowerment Scholarship Program "allows students with special needs an opportunity to receive an education savings account (ESA) funded by the state and administered by an approved scholarship-funding organization (SFO)." Parents can access those accounts and use the funds to pay for "a variety of educational services, including private school tuition, tutoring, online education, home education, curriculum, therapy, postsecondary educational institutions in Florida, and other defined educational services."[112]

It must be said that some homeschool advocates, such as Mike Donnelly, worry that government funding comes with government strings, which could compromise the independence of the homeschooling sector. That is certainly true, as California's efforts to undermine homeschool charter schools show.

However, the financial reality for parents like Heather Harrison is that without the funding that comes to her and her children through the charter school they would never have been able to afford the enrichment classes that make up such an important part of her kids' homeschool experience.

"Charter school, in particular, offers the choice to lower socioeconomic families, such as my husband and I," Harrison says.

Mike Donnelly also urges that homeschooling advocates fight for the principle of parental choice and for fair treatment. "Homeschoolers shouldn't be treated differently from other high school graduates for the purposes of employment, getting into the military, or getting into college," he argues. HSLDA fights against unequal treatment of homeschoolers, "and we do that across all 50 states and we have been increasingly successful in doing that."

Looking around the United States, Donnelly says that many states have actually improved their homeschooling laws over the last two decades. "So we're not seeing a retrenchment," but rather, "continuous revision and improvement of homeschool laws."

"In the U.S. we have relatively good regulations," he observes, "and we want to keep it that way." He warns that homeschooling in European countries is much more regulated. In Germany, for example, people are prosecuted for homeschooling their children.

While things are better in the U.S., Donnelly warns that the homeschooling movement cannot be complacent. Paraphrasing Ronald Reagan, he says, "freedom is not passed in the bloodstream to the next generation." Rather, "it has to be won and fought for every step of the way."

While there may be some disagreement among advocates about the best way forward for homeschooling, McDonald says that this diverse movement is united on basic principles:

> There are very few movements today that bring together such a diverse group of people as homeschooling does. Families of all political persuasions, from all corners of the country, reflecting many different races, ethnicities, classes, cultures, values, and ideologies, and representing a multitude of different learning philosophies and approaches choose homeschooling for the educational freedom and flexibility it provides. Homeschoolers may not agree on much, but preserving the freedom to raise and educate their children as they choose is a unifying priority. In times of division, homeschoolers offer hope and optimism that liberty will prevail.[113]

In fact, the experiences of the parents, children, and educators profiled in this book underscore not only the diversity that McDonald describes, but also the unifying principles that she says bind together these diverse people.

In the end, "Government doesn't know best," says McDonald, "Families know best."[114] This principle undergirds all the personal stories in this book.

Magda Gomez knew better than any government official that homeschooling was the best answer to the bullying her girls experienced in their public school.

Louisa knew better than any government official that Theodore's special needs were best addressed at home, not in a one-size-fits-all public school.

And 12-year-old Justin Chaney knew better than any government official that he would not be happy in a public school that would make him read books about superheroes when he wanted to read Solzhenitsyn's *The Gulag Archipelago*.

The ultimate recommendation for policymakers, therefore, should be this: listen to reason, listen to reality, and, most of all, listen to the voices of parents and students.

ENDNOTES

1   Eric Wearne, "Hybrid Homes Schools and Civil Society," *The Imaginative Conservative*, July 31, 2020, available at https://theimaginativeconservative.org/2020/07/hybrid-home-schools-civil-society-eric-wearne.html

2   Ibid.

3   Ibid.

4   Ibid.

5   Ibid.

6   Ibid.

7   Pia Ceres, "They Rage—Quit the School System—and They're Not Going Back," *Wired.com*, June 3, 2021, available at https://www.wired.com/story/pandemic-homeschoolers-who-are-not-going-back/

8   Ibid.

9   Robin Lake and Travis Pillow, "Analysis: What a new report reveals about the evolving world of homeschooling—and how it could become a laboratory for the future of education," *LA School Report*, July 22, 2019, available at http://laschoolreport.com/analysis-what-a-new-report-reveals-about-the-evolving-world-of-homeschooling-and-how-it-could-become-a-laboratory-for-the-future-of-education/

10 Aaron Hirsh, "The Changing Landscape of Homeschooling in the United States," Center on Reinventing Public Education, University of Washington Bothell, July 2019, available at https://www.crpe.org/sites/default/files/homeschooling_brief_final.pdf

11 Casey Eggleston and Jason Fields, "Census Bureau's Household Pulse Survey Shows Significant Increase in Homeschooling Rates in Fall 2020," United States Census Bureau, March 22, 2021, available at https://www.census.gov/library/stories/2021/03/homeschooling-on-the-rise-during-covid-19-pandemic.html

12 Dave Dentel, "Census Data Shows Phenomenal Homeschool Growth," Homeschool Legal Defense Association, April 13, 2021, available at https://hslda.org/post/census-data-shows-phenomenal-homeschool-growth

13 Casey Eggleston and Jason Fields, op. cit.

14 Ibid.

15 Ibid.

16 Joy Pullman, "Homeschooling Skyrocketed In 2020, As Much As 700 Percent In Some States," *The Federalist*, June 1, 2021, available at https://thefederalist.com/2021/06/01/homeschooling-skyrocketed-in-2020-as-much-as-700-percent-in-some-states/

17 Casey Eggleston and Jason Fields, op. cit.

18 Ibid.

19 Kathleen Bustamante, "Rise of the Homeschool Mom," *The American Conservative*, June 26, 2021, available at https://www.theamericanconservative.com/articles/rise-of-the-homeschool-mom/

20 Ibid.

21 Emma Dorn, Bryan Hancock, Jimmy Sarakatsannis, and Ellen Viruleg, "COVID-19 and education: The lingering effects of unfinished learning," McKinsey & Company, July 27, 2021, available at https://www.mckinsey.com/industries/public-and-social-sector/our-insights/covid-19-and-education-the-lingering-effects-of-unfinished-learning

22 Ibid.

23 "CREDO at Stanford University Presents Estimates of Learning Loss in the 2019-2020 School Year," CREDO at Stanford University, October 1, 2020, available at https://www.prnewswire.com/news-releases/credo-at-stanford-university-presents-estimates-of-learning-loss-in-the-2019-2020-school-year-301144363.html

24 Vladimir Kogan and Stephane Laveru, "The COVID-19 Pandemic and Student Achievement on Ohio's Third Grade Englsh Language Arts Assesment," The Ohio State University, January 27, 2021, p. 1, available at http://glenn.osu.edu/educational-governance/reports/reports-attributes/ODE_ThirdGradeELA_KL_1-27-2021.pdf

25 Libby Pier, Heather Hough, Michael Christian, Noah Bookman, Britt Wilkenfield, and Rick Miller, "COVID-19 and the Educational Equity Crisis," Policy Analysis for California Education (PACE), January 25, 2021, available at https://edpolicyinca.org/newsroom/covid-19-and-educational-equity-crisis

26 Ibid.

27 Ibid.

28 "Thirty four percent of eighth-graders at or above NAEP Proficient lower than 2017," NAEP Report Card: Reading, available at https://www.nationsreportcard.gov/reading/nation/achievement/?grade=8

29 "Sixty-ning percent of students at or above NAEP Basic lower compared to 2017," NAEP Report Card: Mathematics, available at https://www.nationsreportcard.gov/mathematics/nation/achievement/?grade=8

30 Lindsey Burke, "Bringing Achievement Home: A Review of the Academic Outcomes of Homeschooling Students in the United States," Home School Legal Defense Association, 2019, p. 6, available at https://secureservercdn.net/45.40.149.34/n5e.cd2.myftpupload.com/wp-content/uploads/2020/04/Bringing-Achievment-Home.pdf

31 Ibid, pp. 17-18.

32 Ibid, p. 18.

33 Ibid, p. 4.

34 "Homeschooling in the United States: Results from the 2012 and 2016 Parent and Family involvement Survey (PFI-NHES: 2012 and 2016)," United States Department of Education, December 2019, p. 8, available at https://files.eric.ed.gov/fulltext/ED601971.pdf

35   Chris Weller, "Homeschooling could be the smartest way to teach kids in the 21st century—here are 5 reasons why," *Business Insider*, January 18, 2018, available at https://www. businessinsider.com/reasons-homeschooling-is-the-smartest-way-to-teach-kids-today-2018-1?op=1#schooling-isnt-set-apart-from-the-real-world-5

36   Robin Lake and Travis Pillow, op. cit.

37   Pia Ceres, op. cit.

38   Dave Dentel, op. cit.

39   Casey Eggleston and Jason Fields, op. cit.

40   Ibid.

41   Vladimir Kogan and Stephane Laveru, op. cit., p. 1.

42   Alison Yoshimoto-Towery and Pedro Garcia, "Additional Time for Students to Increase Proficiency—Fall 2020 Grades," Los Angeles Unified School District Division of Instruction, Interoffice Correspondence, available at https:// assets.documentcloud.org/documents/20424082/20-12-14-additional-time-to-reach-proficiency.pdf

43   "74 Interview: Professor Cheryl Fields-Smith on Why More Black Families are Homeschooling Their Kids," *The 74*, April 2, 2017, available at https://www.the74million.org/article/74-interview-professor-cheryl-fields-smith-on-why-more-black-families-are-homeschooling-their-kids/

44   Ibid.

45   Ibid.

46   Ron Matus, "Hispanic Homeschoolers on the Rise," *redefinED*, February 27, 2020, available at https://www.redefinedonline. org/2020/02/hispanic-homeschoolers-on-the-rise/

47   Ibid.

48   Ibid.

49   See https://www.mommymaestra.com/p/about-me.html

50   See https://www.mommymaestra.com/2020/07/hispanic-bilingual-homeschoolers.html

51 Ron Matus, op. cit.

52 See https://www3.cde.ca.gov/psa/

53 Camille Kirksey, "10 Black Homeschool Moms You Should Follow," Mater Mea, available at https://matermea.com/10-black-homeschool-moms-you-should-follow/

54 Ibid.

55 See http://momzest.com

56 Karen Andreola, "I Call Charlotte Mason's Philosophy and Method the Gentle Art of Learning," charlottemason.com, available at https://charlottemason.com/the-gentle-art-of-learning/

57 See https://www.classicalconversations.com/about/

58 See https://www.youtube.com/watch?v=1BEvhZIe-rQ&t=211s

59 "The Homeschooling Experience: Focus Groups with Homeschooling and Personalized Learning Parents," EdChoice, June 23, 2021, p. 17, available at https://www.edchoice.org/wp-content/uploads/2021/06/Homeschool-Personalized-Learning-FG.pdf

60 Ibid, p. 23.

61 Ibid.

62 Jackie Nunes, "Why I Broke Up With My School District to Homeschool My Child With Special Needs," *Education Post*, October 5, 2018, available at https://educationpost.org/i-broke-up-school-district-homeschool-child-special-needs/

63 Ibid.

64 Ibid.

65 Ibid.

66 "Hyposensitivity to Touch and Movement: Definition and Overview," Study.com, available at https://study.com/academy/lesson/hyposensitivity-to-touch-movement-definition-lesson-quiz.html

67   Erin O'Donnell, "The Risks of Homeschooling,"
     Harvard Magazine, May-June 2020, available at https://
     www.harvardmagazine.com/2020/05/right-now-risks-
     homeschooling

68   Brian Ray, "Homeschooling: The Research," National Home
     Education Research Institute, May 3, 2021, available at
     https://www.nheri.org/research-facts-on-homeschooling/

69   Kathleen Bustamante, op. cit.

70   Tommy Schultz, "National Poll: 40% of Families More
     Likely to Homeschool After Lockdowns End," RealClear
     Opinion Research, May 14, 2020, available at https://www.
     federationforchildren.org/national-poll-40-of-families-more-
     likely-to-homeschool-after-lockdowns-end/

71   Jeanne Faulconer, "What is a Homeschool Co-op?",
     TheHomeSchoolMom.com, available at https://www.
     thehomeschoolmom.com/what-is-homeschool-co-op/

72   See https://susanwisebauer.com/well-trained-mind/

73   Michael Shaw, "2020 Schooling in America Series:
     Homeschooling Experiences and Views During the
     Pandemic," EdChoice, August 8, 2020, available at https://
     www.edchoice.org/engage/2020-schooling-in-america-series-
     homeschooling-experiences-and-views-during-the-pandemic/

74   Jack Lebraque, "Homeschooling on the rise across Oregon,"
     KATU-TV, August 24, 2018, available at https://katu.com/
     news/local/homeschooling-on-the-rise-across-oregon

75   Valerie Richardson, "Homeschooling surges as parents seek
     escape from shootings, violence," *The Washington Times,* May
     30, 2018, available at https://www.washingtontimes.com/
     news/2018/may/30/homeschooling-surges-parents-seek-
     escape-shootings/

76   "Restorative Justice in the Schools," School Counselors
     Connect, see http://schoolcounselorsconnect.weebly.com/
     restorative-justice.html

77   See https://www.publiccharters.org/about-charter-schools/
     what-charter-school

78 See https://www.time4learning.com/homeschooling/california/charter-schools.html

79 See https://pact.natomascharter.org

80 Ibid.

81 See https://pact.natomascharter.org/pf4/cms2/view_page?d=x&group_id=1524554865023&vdid=i1g3g1uo11ra

82 See the services offered by one umbrella school at https://www.freshedhomeschool.com/psp

83 See https://ogcs.org/og-premium-content/og-if/og-if-amounts?fbclid=IwAR26KKfsO0uQWwykbnui3n7lmuTixXQ_2nB_mURGzrQWMeOV-aFVOtpLQOE

84 See https://ogcs.org/og-parentinformation/og-parent-faq#How_does_school_funding_work?

85 Ibid.

86 Kerry McDonald, *Unschooled* (Chicago, IL: Chicago Review Press, 2019), p. 26.

87 Ibid, p. 27.

88 Ibid, p. v.

89 Ibid.

90 Ibid, p. 20.

91 Ibid, p. 36.

92 Eric Todisco, "Kris Jenner Opens Up About Kendall and Kylie's Homeschooling Experience," *People*, September 26, 2019, available at https://people.com/tv/kris-jenner-opens-up-kendall-jenner-kylie-jenner-homeschooling-experience/

93 See https://noveleducationgroup.com

94 Ibid.

95 Eric Todisco, op. cit.

96 Elizabeth Bartholet, "Homeschooling: Parent Rights Absolutism vs. Child Rights to Education and Protection," *Arizona Law Review*, Vol. 62:1 2020, pp. 72-73, available at https://arizonalawreview.org/pdf/62-1/62arizlrev1.pdf

97 Brian Ray, "Child Abuse of Public School, Private School, and Homeschool Students: Evidence, Philosophy, and Reason," National Home Education Research Institute, January 23, 2018, available at https://www.nheri.org/child-abuse-of-public-school-private-school-and-homeschool-students-evidence-philosophy-and-reason/

98 Kerry McDonald, "Harvard Prof Asks Biden to 'Reform our Current Homeschooling Regime.' Here's the Problem With Her Proposal," Foundation for Economic Education, May 11, 2021, available at https://fee.org/articles/harvard-prof-asks-biden-to-reform-our-current-homeschooling-regime-here-s-the-problem-with-her-proposal/

99 Brian Ray, op. cit.

100 "Percentage of Public Schools Recording Incidents of Crime at School and Reporting Incidents to Police, Number of Incidents, and Rate per 1,000 Students, by Type of Crime: Selected years, 1999-2000 through 2017-18," National Center for Education Statistics, 2019, available at https://nces.ed.gov/programs/digest/d19/tables/dt19_229.10.asp

101 Ibid.

102 Ibid.

103 Kristen Schmitt, "Is Your Child the Bully or the Bullied?," *USA Today*, August 10, 2019, https://www.usatoday.com/story/life/2019/08/10/stop-bullying/1965145001/

104 Elizabeth Bartholet, op. cit., p. 73.

105 "Evaluating President Biden's first 100 days: Children and families," *Harvard Law Today*, April 30, 2021, available at https://today.law.harvard.edu/evaluating-president-bidens-first-100-days-children-and-families/

106 Larry Sand, "Pandemic Pod Pushback," California Policy Center, November 10, 2020, available at https://californiapolicycenter.org/pandemic-pod-pushback/

107 "2011 National Education Association Resolutions," available at https://web.archive.org/web/20130806000606/ https:/peiowa.org/wp-content/uploads/2011/03/NEA_ Resolutions_2011.pdf

108 Elliott Kaufman, "The Teachers Union's Tiny New Enemy," *The Wall Street Journal*, October 14, 2020, available at https://www.wsj.com/articles/the-teachers-unions-tiny-new-enemy-11602709305

109 Eric Spitznagel, "Parents are giving up on public schools to home-school their kids," *New York Post*, October 12, 2018, available at https://nypost.com/2018/10/12/parents-are-abandoning-public-schools-in-droves-to-homeschool-their-kids/

110 See https://leginfo.legislature.ca.gov/faces/billTextClient.xhtml?bill_id=201920200SB820

111 Kerry McDonald, "'Pandemic Pods' Make Homeschooling Easier For Parents and Profitable for Teachers," Foundation for Economic Education, July 23, 2020, available at https://fee.org/articles/pandemic-pods-make-homeschooling-easier-for-parents-and-profitable-for-teachers/

112 "Florida Empowerment Scholarship Program," EdChoice, see https://www.edchoice.org/school-choice/programs/gardiner-scholarship-program/

113 Kerry McDonald, "5 Things I Learned Debating the Harvard Prof Who Called for a 'Presumptive Ban' on Homeschooling," Foundation for Economic Education, June 19, 2020, available at https://fee.org/articles/5-things-i-learned-debating-the-harvard prof who called-for-a-presumptive-ban-on-homeschooling/

114 Kerry McDonald, "'Pandemic Pods' Make Homeschooling Easier for Parents and Profitable for Teachers," op. cit.

ACKNOWLEDGEMENTS

Many people assisted in the preparation of this book. The author would like to thank: Cecilia Iglesias, Rebecca Friedrichs, Abbess Isihia, Dr. Ting Sun, and Brandi Jordania Goldberg. In addition, the author would like to thank Christine Zanello and Mia Giordano for introducing the author into the world of homeschooling.

The author would also like to thank Pacific Research Institute president and CEO Sally Pipes, PRI senior vice president Rowena Itchon, and PRI communications director Tim Anaya for editing this book (any remaining errors or omissions are the sole responsibility of the authors), graphic designer Dana Beigel, PRI vice president of development Ben Smithwick, and the other dedicated PRI staff who made this book possible.

The author of this book worked independently. His views and conclusions do not necessarily represent those of the board, supporters, and staff of PRI.

ABOUT THE AUTHOR

Lance Izumi is Senior Director of the Center for Education at the Pacific Research Institute. He has written and produced books, studies and films on a wide variety of education topics. Most recently, he is the author of the 2019 book *Choosing Diversity: How Charter Schools Promote Diverse Learning Models and Meet the Diverse Needs of Parents and Children* and the 2020 book *A Kite in a Hurricane No More: One Woman's Journey Overcoming Learning Disabilities through Science and Educational Choice."*

He is a two-term president of the Board of Governors of the California Community Colleges, the largest system of higher education in the nation, and served as a member of the Board from 2004 to 2015.

From 2015 to 2018, Lance chaired the board of directors of the Foundation for California Community Colleges, the official non-profit that supports the community college system, and remains a member of the board.

Lance served as a commissioner on the California Postsecondary Education Commission and as a member of the United States Civil Rights Commission's California Advisory Committee.

Lance served as chief speechwriter and director of writing and research for California Governor George Deukmejian and as speechwriter to United States Attorney General Edwin Meese III in President Ronald Reagan's administration.

Lance received his Juris Doctorate from the University of Southern California School of Law, his Master of Arts in political science from the University of California at Davis, and his Bachelor of Arts in economics and history from the University of California at Los Angeles.

ABOUT PACIFIC RESEARCH INSTITUTE

The Pacific Research Institute (PRI) champions freedom, opportunity, and personal responsibility by advancing free-market policy solutions. It provides practical solutions for the policy issues that impact the daily lives of all Americans, and demonstrates why the free market is more effective than the government at providing the important results we all seek: good schools, quality health care, a clean environment, and a robust economy.

Founded in 1979 and based in San Francisco, PRI is a non-profit, non-partisan organization supported by private contributions. Its activities include publications, public events, media commentary, community leadership, legislative testimony, and academic outreach.

CENTER FOR BUSINESS AND ECONOMICS
PRI shows how the entrepreneurial spirit—the engine of economic growth and opportunity—is stifled by onerous taxes, regulations, and lawsuits. It advances policy reforms that promote a robust economy, consumer choice, and innovation.

CENTER FOR EDUCATION
PRI works to restore to all parents the basic right to choose the best educational opportunities for their children. Through research and grassroots outreach, PRI promotes parental choice in education, high academic standards, teacher quality, charter schools, and school-finance reform.

CENTER FOR THE ENVIRONMENT
PRI reveals the dramatic and long-term trend toward a cleaner, healthier environment. It also examines and promotes the essential ingredients for abundant resources and environmental quality: property rights, markets, local action, and private initiative.

CENTER FOR HEALTH CARE
PRI demonstrates why a single-payer Canadian model would be detrimental to the health care of all Americans. It proposes market-based reforms that would improve affordability, access, quality, and consumer choice.

CENTER FOR CALIFORNIA REFORM
The Center for California Reform seeks to reinvigorate California's entrepreneurial self-reliant traditions. It champions solutions in education, business, and the environment that work to advance prosperity and opportunity for all the state's residents.

CENTER FOR MEDICAL ECONOMICS AND INNOVATION
The Center for Medical Economics and Innovation aims to educate policymakers, regulators, health care professionals, the media, and the public on the critical role that new technologies play in improving health and accelerating economic growth.

The Homeschool Boom